CHURCHES OF VISION

Stories from the Five Jurisdictions of United Methodism

Ralph and Nell Mohney

P.O. Box 189 • Nashville, TN 37202 • Phone (615) 340-7284

CONTENTS

ABOUT THIS BOOK

A plethora of books, articles, addresses, and sermons depicting the plight of The United Methodist Church and other major denominations has captured our attention. We have heard the dire predictions detailing the not too distant demise of the denomination. Fortunately, other voices have pointed out that our church is not one great ship on the sea of twentieth-century life. Rather, The United Methodist Church is like a great flotilla of ships, and each local church charts its own course. Although many churches are sailing into oblivion, many others are turning from such a fate through spiritual renewal. Such churches are steaming in the direction for which the church was created with unsurpassed vigor and vitality.

The General Board of Discipleship is perhaps more acutely aware of modern-day trends than is any other body within the structure of the church; thus, the board seeks to relate to the needs of churches in as many ways as possible. Recently, the board has added another facet to its multifaceted ministry, namely, the "large-membership church initiative," which attempts to meet the needs of churches that have an average Sunday morning worship attendance of 350 or more or a total membership of 1,000 or more. As a result of the work of this initiative, the video, *Leading the Large Membership Church: The Senior Pastor*, was mailed to all senior pastors of these churches; conferences for newly appointed senior pastors are being conducted; conferences for senior pastors of churches of varying size memberships are being planned; and teaching churches are being identified.

As adjunct staff members of the General Board of Discipleship, we were asked to find churches in each of the five Jurisdictions of United Methodism whose ministries could be described in words reflecting the working of God in our contemporary setting. Names of the fastest growing churches in each of the five jurisdictions for 1980–1985 were compiled by the board's Office of Research. These churches are among those having the largest numerical increases in membership during those years. They range from 228 net increase in a church in the Northeastern Jurisdiction to 2,038 net increase in a church in the South Central Jurisdiction, and from the number one, or fastest growing church to the number 211th among all 37,800 churches.

Each of these "churches of vision" is distinctive in its history, its setting, and its focus of ministry. These churches represent newly formed churches, churches more than a hundred years old, downtown churches, suburban churches, and newly developed community churches. Wide variations exist among the jurisdictions, but each account tells that wherever the churches are located and whatever their pasts may have been, they have demonstrated their ability to respond to God's call, reach out to their communities, and find increasing numbers of people who need that which the churches feel God has called them to offer.

We hope that this brief account will not only help focus attention on the positive side of what God is doing in the church, but that it will provide insight and incentive to enable other congregations to become "churches of vision."

RALPH AND NELL MOHNEY

NORTHEASTERN JURISDICTION

A. P. SHAW UNITED METHODIST CHURCH

WASHINGTON, D.C.

*E. W. Stevenson, Sr., Senior Pastor**

Everett Stevenson *is* A. P. Shaw United Methodist Church in the minds of its members. Stevenson does not do all of the work or run the church single-handedly. Quite the opposite is true. The percentage of lay involvement is far higher than in most churches we have observed. Every member at Shaw Church is involved and has a definite sense of ownership for how the church is going.

The inability of the members to separate the man from the message means that he is so close to them personally and has done so much for the church during its 41 years since he established it as a Sunday school for children in 1949. The story of its beginning is as inspiring as its current story of growth and mission.

As a young married man with two small children, Stevenson was working in the District of Columbia. Though his parents and grandparents were Christians and active members of the Methodist Church, Stevenson, like many of his peers, dropped out of high school and out of church during his teen years. Also like his peers, he became a problem drinker. His weekends were filled with carousing, drinking, fighting, and spending all of his paycheck.

One Sunday evening he suddenly realized that he was on a journey going nowhere. If he continued the way he was going, he would kill someone or be killed himself, and his wife and children would have nothing. He decided to enlist in the Marines. At least if he were killed there, his young family would have some financial security. Stationed on Guam, his drinking continued, even worsened. In fact, on

---

*Bernard Keels became senior pastor of A. P. Shaw United Methodist Church in 1990.

the day of the Japanese surrender, many Marines celebrated for 24 hours with alcohol, but Stevenson stayed drunk
for a week. When he came to, he had a terrible pain in his
heart, as if a heavy hand were pushing against it.

The doctors in the medical unit could find no physical cause
for the pain. Stevenson felt in a deep, intuitive way that it was
God's hand on his heart, and he literally ran to the bamboo
chapel on the island and made a commitment of his life to Jesus
Christ. The pain eased. From that day in 1945 to today, he has
not had a drink of alcoholic beverages.

Back home in the States, Stevenson experienced the same
pain when he thought about his vocation, and checked with a
cardiologist in Washington, D.C. The medical opinion was that
his heart was as "sound as a dollar." His mother-in-law suggested that God was calling him into the ministry.

Though Stevenson had suspected this, he had fought against
it. When he finally said, "Yes," he was overwhelmed with such
a feeling of peace and joy that he began to shout. The indwell-
ing of the Holy Spirit still is evident in his countenance and his
persuasive preaching.

When Stevenson talked to the district superintendent of the
Methodist Church, he was told to come back in seven years,
after he had completed his high school, college, and seminary
training. Though disappointed, he started to high school at
night, while serving as a mail carrier during the day. Even so,
he was burning with a desire to serve God, so he began a
Sunday school with ten children who lived in the housing
project where he and his family lived.

At first, the group met in a dilapidated, rented building on
the bank of a creek. The Sunday school grew, but the building
was soon washed away during a flash flood. That event proved
to be a blessing in disguise. A reporter from the *Washington
Post* wrote an article about Stevenson's dreams for the children
and about his disappointment. The story touched the hearts of
many residents of the District of Columbia, and money began
to come in for the construction of a permanent building. At the
same time, mothers, who were grateful for what the Sunday
school meant to their children, began to get involved, and the
Methodist Church voted to pay Everett $40.00 a month for his
ministry. A. P. Shaw United Methodist Church (named for a
bishop of the former Central Jurisdiction) was on its way. It

was two years, however, before the first man came to the church.

Today, the attractive church and its educational building are still located in the housing project and built on what was called "Old Whiskey Dump." Strong male, as well as female, leadership is evident in the membership of 1,700. Some of the children from that first Sunday school have grown up to become well-educated, successful professionals who have moved out of the project into more affluent neighborhoods. Still, they retain their membership and leadership in the church that did so much for them. They agree with their pastor that the best protection young people can have against drugs and their attendant evils includes a personal commitment to Christ, a strong family, and a vital church relationship.

Tithing of money, time, and talents is a strong emphasis of the church. As a result, the pastor is the only paid staff member. Volunteerism is high and well organized. An especially important program, which adds significantly to the stability of the church, is the membership class. Every adult who joins the church on profession of faith or transfer of membership is required to take a six-week membership class on what it means to be a Christian and what it means to be a United Methodist. In addition, they have to pass a test before they are certified members. Membership, thus, becomes a real commitment.

This fastest growing church of the Northeastern Jurisdiction is characterized by strong evangelistic worship services, lay visitation, good music (five choirs with instrumentalists), Sunday school, an athletic program for children and youth, and social outreach. In addition to a food pantry and clothes closet for the needy of the neighborhood, the men of the church have worked with the mayor in scheduling "Operation Clean Sweep" to rid their housing project of drug dealers. Southeast Washington is one of the worst areas for heavy drug traffic and crimes of vandalism and violence. In the midst of this evil stands Shaw United Methodist Church, like a lighthouse atop which the lighted cross symbolizes "release of the captives and recovery of sight for those who have lost their way."

FIRST UNITED METHODIST CHURCH

LIVERPOOL, NEW YORK

James LeGro and Everett Bassett, Pastors

How do you visit one of the five fastest growing churches of the Northeastern Jurisdiction when its town, Liverpool, New York, is not listed on the usual travel maps? Even learning that the village of Liverpool is a part of the township of Salina doesn't help because Salina is not on many maps either. The task becomes more difficult when the traveler learns that the village of Liverpool has a population of 3,000 persons today and First United Methodist Church has a membership of 3,200. How did all this happen?

First, in the greater Liverpool area are a number of villages and small towns that serve as bedroom communities for the city of Syracuse, for a group of nearby industries such as General Electric and General Motors, and for corporate headquarters of companies like Mony. For many years Allied Chemical was the only industry in the Liverpool area. Allied came to the state because of the nearby Onondaga Lake and the salt mines. The area is much stronger today because of the diversity of industry and because Interstate 81 runs north and south and the east-west Interstate 70 converges there. An indication of the growth is found in the population statistics. In 1957 in the greater Liverpool area there were 27,000 residents; in 1989 the number had grown to 47,000. In the village itself the population went from 1,000 to 3,000.

First United Methodist Church in Liverpool was a strong congregation of 1,100 members in 1964. The large numerical growth came under the 25-year pastoral leadership of Milton Jefferson. He was truly God's man at the right place at the right time.

Natives of New England, Milton and Shirley were married when he was enrolled at Boston University School of

Theology. After graduation, they decided they would like to serve in another conference and state, but not too far from their families. They chose North Central New York. After two very successful pastorates, Jefferson was appointed to First Church Liverpool.

Although it's true that he arrived during a time of population growth, it is also true that other Protestant churches and certainly other United Methodist churches grew little or not at all during this time. Jefferson's strategy for growth was simple but effective. His overarching philosophy maintains that a church grows when individual members are continuously deepening their commitment to Jesus Christ. His two areas of focus for accomplishing this were inspiring worship services and solid Christian education, especially through the Sunday school for all ages, including adults.

The worship services, which grew from one 11:00 A.M. service when he arrived in 1964 to three morning services (8:00, 9:30, and 11:00) in 1989, were all traditional. He wore a clerical collar and robe. He had no hymns announced and no announcements made during worship, a practice that helped to signify the importance and holiness of worship. Though the services were formal, they were never stiff or boring. In the easy flow of the service, feeling was emphasized in music (both choral and congregational) and in the reading of the Word, and the focus was on the sermon.

Marshall McLuhan wrote a book declaring that the "medium is the message." It's easy to see where this has been true with Jefferson. He has a pleasant face and marvelous voice. With his well-controlled voice, he could paint graphic word pictures and create excitement or silence. In addition, he made preaching a priority, so he was always well prepared. The sermon was finished a week before he preached it, and he practiced it for six days. His sermon became so much a part of him that he had no need to use notes, could easily and naturally incorporate current happenings of interest to the congregation, and could be open to the leadership of the Holy Spirit. He compared this to radio waves that pick up what is said, enlarge it, and send it great distances. So, he believed, a preacher who is well prepared can be more open to the Holy Spirit, who expands the message and carries it to the deep recesses of the human heart.

Jefferson's sermons were Christ-centered and life-oriented. They were not prophetic sermons, but he encouraged individuals to live out their faith in service in the church, the community, and the world.

In the early days of population growth, Jefferson called on every new family who moved into the area. His wife, Shirley, laughingly called him a moving-van chaser. As a result, 90 percent of the current membership comes from outside Liverpool, many driving 10 to 20 miles in order to attend church there. Today, the members extend invitations to newcomers, and the membership committee has all it can do to follow up on first-time visitors.

Another plus of Jefferson's ministry was his ability to get people with manual skills (electricians, plumbers, carpenters) to use those skills in the church, thus saving the congregation large amounts of money, which could be used for ministry. Working together also provided fellowship and camaraderie among the members. For example, when the sanctuary needed painting, people of the church did it while others were there to serve sandwiches, coffee, and desserts. Everybody had fun sharing a common task.

That philosophy of working together continues. Every Saturday morning a group of men known as the "Saturday Phew" meet to perform needed repairs and renovations or to supplement the work of the custodian. Another evidence of this spirit is that every adult group in the church—Sunday school classes, circles, choirs, commissions—take turns providing "Sunday night supper" for the youth of the church.

In the area of finances, Jefferson established a legacy program, which provides an endowment fund, the interest on which provides capital funds for such projects as renovation and purchasing a new organ. In connection with this, a long-range planning committee has been buying adjacent properties for needed expansion of the facilities.

Jefferson retired at the June 1989 meeting of the North Central New York Conference. Yet his philosophy of ministry is firmly etched on the large congregation he leaves behind. The staff, lay leadership, and congregation compose a strongly evangelical church in the finest sense of that word. They are deeply committed Christians and serve out of a love for Christ and not out of a sense of duty. They are not fundamentalists, but live out their belief in the fundamentals of the Christian faith.

The church has a well-orchestrated, though not tightly structured, commitment to authentic caring for any who are hurting—members and non-members alike. James Spear, who was appointed to succeed Jefferson, and his family were recipients of that caring. Immediately after his appointment, Spear discovered that he had a serious illness, requiring many days of hospitalization. He returned to the pulpit only briefly before his death. Throughout his illness and during his family's difficult period of transition, the congregation demonstrated sensitivity, love, and personal support.

The months during which Spear was ill and after his death, Everett Bassett, the associate pastor, was given compassionate support and energetic assistance by many members as he guided this congregation through a difficult transition. Then, for the second time in less than a year, a new senior pastor, James LeGro, was appointed and assumed his leadership role.

LeGro's goals are the same as his predecessors. He wants to assist the members of the congregation to realize their dreams of enhancing their spiritual growth, enlarging the physical plant, increasing social outreach, building a stronger financial base, and increasing the involvement of members. Because of the strong history of this congregation and the strength of commitment and caring demonstrated during this difficult transition, there is no reason that, with the grace of God, First United Methodist Church in Liverpool, New York, cannot remain the largest church in its episcopal area.

GROVE UNITED METHODIST CHURCH

WEST CHESTER, PENNSYLVANIA

Alan Brown, Senior Pastor

Have you ever heard a great deal about some person or group so that you had pictured them in your mind without ever having actually seen them? Then when you met them, they didn't look at all like the picture in your mind.

Something of the same thing happened when we visited Grove United Methodist Church in West Chester, Pennsylvania. During the years in which many United Methodist churches had declined in membership and some had even closed, Grove Church had grown from 851 in 1980 to 1,160 in 1985. In fact, this was one of the fastest growing churches in the Northeastern Jurisdiction during these years.

Because of the steady growth in membership and attendance, we had pictured Grove Church as a suburban church probably established in the '50s or as a former downtown church that had moved out into a growing suburban area. Imagine our surprise when we drove up to a pastoral setting and found a church that was established by Francis Asbury in 1773. The lovely serpentine stone building, which houses the sanctuary, was built in 1888. In an attempt to provide for the continued growth, members built an educational wing in 1959 with a stone façade to blend aesthetically with the sanctuary. In 1986, the sanctuary was enlarged and a second floor was added to the educational building.

Actually, the members of Grove Church had no choice but to go up with their building because they are landlocked by a very large cemetery on the south and west and a much-traveled road on the north. To the north and east is the parking area, which even now is not sufficient on special Sundays. Many rural churches have an adjacent cemetery, but the cemetery around Grove Church is unusually large.

Despite the pastoral setting, the church has a contemporary suburban feeling with the number and quality of its programs. For example, young mothers bring their children to vacation Bible school, which lasts two weeks. At the last Bible school, there were 232 children ages four through twelve. Their vacation Bible school and the weekday preschool program, with an enrollment of 150 children and a waiting list, are two excellent ports of entry for new members.

Another important port of entry is through a rapidly growing youth program for junior and senior highs. In 1988, the church wisely selected a competent young woman as pastor to youth. She is a committed Christian, well trained in youth ministry and extremely popular with the young people of the church. She has been successful in involving youth and adults in outreach ministries.

We have observed that many long-established churches find it difficult to welcome newcomers and especially to turn over reins of leadership. This is not so at Grove. Out meeting with the lay leadership during a luncheon was an exciting experience. These people not only love their church, but they are future-oriented. They are visionary, flexible, open to change, and committed to the principle of rotation in leadership.

Through their long-range planning committee and their follow-up through the council on ministries and the administrative board, they have programmed well for children, youth, families, and older adults or "Elderberries" as they are called. Their future plans include a singles' ministry and a stronger Sunday school.

None of these things could have happened so smoothly and steadily except for a professional staff that is talented, committed, energetic, and cooperative. Alan Brown began his fourth year in June 1990. His collegial style of leadership commands respect from other members of the staff and enables them to liberate their own strengths. His area of professional strengths includes preaching, counseling, teaching, and administration. Of special concern to him are the three worship experiences on Sunday morning. The services focus on prophetic preaching, exciting music, and an atmosphere of warmth and caring.

Both the minister of music and the organist have filled

their staff positions for over 20 years. There is a chancel or "tabernacle" choir, a youth choir, junior choir, cherub choir, and adult bell choir. In addition to singing for the regular worship services, the tabernacle choir presents a special musical work during Advent and Lent, and the youth perform a contemporary musical during the year.

Barbara Housley has been on the staff as associate pastor for five years. Her background is elementary education and child development. Her expertise is also in camping, older adult ministries, and pastoral concerns. Both pastors have led the congregation in greater involvement in social outreach in the community and around the world. The pastor to youth, two secretaries, one of whom has been on the staff for ten years, another part-time secretary, and a custodian complete the staff. They all model compassionate caring and are truly having a team ministry.

In summary, we believe this interesting church has grown and continues to grow because of visibility, competent lay leaders who are visionary and open to change, excellent staff who work together well, balanced programming, and vital worship. If they continue to focus on these strengths and are as willing to move from medium size to a large church as they were from a rural to a suburban church and if they stay firmly rooted in their belief that they can meet any challenge with God's help, Grove United Methodist Church will be like a light that is set upon a hill to bring Christ's light and hope to the people of West Chester, Pennsylvania, and others around the world.

KENT ISLAND UNITED METHODIST CHURCH

KENT ISLAND, MARYLAND

*David Weber, Senior Pastor**

A bridge built; a future envisioned; a merger completed; a growing church. In brief, this is the history of Kent Island United Methodist Church. Located across the Chesapeake Bay from Annapolis, Maryland, Kent Island is a fast-growing community—from 5,000 residents in 1980 to 15,000 in 1989.

For many years, only the hard-working natives lived on the island, most of whom were fishermen with their families. Until 1951, when the Bay Bridge was completed, Kent Island provided very simple living—no supermarket, no dry cleaner, no fast-food restaurant, no shopping mall.

Methodism on the island goes back to August 1778 when Freeborn Garrettson preached there and found a class meeting already organized. Francis Asbury and Thomas Coke had preached and established the class in 1774. The current Kent Island United Methodist Church occupies a beautiful colonial brick building on a 10-acre plot, strategically located for easy visibility for all who cross the Bay Bridge from the mainland. United Methodism is indebted to those visionary Peninsula Conference leaders who recognized the inevitability of population growth following the building of the bridge. They not only purchased the property but also assisted in the merger of three small Methodist churches—Trinity Downes, Kingsley, and Dominion. The merger was complete, and the present Kent Island United Methodist Church was incorporated in 1960. The sanctuary and office building were finished in 1963, and the education building, including classrooms, kitchen, and fellowship hall, was ready for occupancy in 1973.

**David Weber moved to Chestnut Street United Methodist Church in Portland, Maine, effective July 1, 1990.*

In the meantime, Annapolis had become a bedroom community for the nation's capital. As houses continued to rise in desirability and cost, the first wave of new residents moved to Kent Island in the early 1960s. Since then they have continued to come. The one deterrent to growth has been the community's inability to provide services as fast as needed. Today, this problem is being addressed, and continued growth is expected.

Being at the right place at the right time is one of the reasons Kent Island United Methodist Church was one of the fastest growing churches in the Northeastern Jurisdiction from 1980 to 1985. Yet several other churches, Protestant and Catholic, which were located nearby, did not grow proportionately to the island's population growth. Some of the reasons for this church's continued growth include intentionality about growth; intentionality about having a "full service" church; commitment to being the "Body of Christ"; and an excellent staff and a large corps of lay volunteers. Let's look at these.

First, their being intentional about growth is evident. They have a careful and thorough follow-up on each first-time visitor to their weekly services of worship—letters from both pastors, telephone calls, lay visitation, lay and personal visits by the senior pastor. Also, leaders never say the church is too big or express a wish that they might stay the size they are. The senior pastor, David Weber, showed us their long-range planning chart, indicating the projected growth of Kent Island and the church for the years 1990, 2000, and 2005. At present, the island population is under the projection, and the church membership is over the projection.

Second, there is a commitment to "find a need and meet it; find a hurt and heal it." They have programmed for all age groups in worship, education, fellowship, and outreach. Because the church membership is made up of persons who grew up in varied denominations and faiths, the congregation is a "mixed bag," theologically. They have programmed for this in an 8:30 A.M. worship experience that is informal and open in terms of worship style. Participants in this worship take time to share joys and sorrows and to request prayers. Also, there is less ritual, and hymns are requested by the members from the *Family of God* hymnal.

At 11:00 A.M. the service is much more traditional, and the congregation seems to be divided equally in number between the two services. Music is an exciting part of both services. Sunday school classes are provided for all ages—nursery through adults. The church is recognized for its ministry to children and youth. In addition, small groups include Bible study, prayer groups, mothers' fellowship groups, men's prayer breakfast group, United Methodist Women, United Methodist Men, and a year-long confirmation class.

Third, there is a strong spiritual undertone to the congregation. The church seems genuinely to desire to be a part of the "Body of Christ." It is a praying congregation and a caring congregation. The Stephen's ministry has mobilized many laypersons and trained them, under the able direction of Sandra Ball, to become lay ministers for members who are hurting. Living out the principles of Christ includes local outreach such as a food closet for the hungry and mission projects to Appalachia and the Navajo Indians.

Fourth, Weber and Ball seem to be a balanced, complementary pastoral team, and they lead an excellent staff and a large corps of lay volunteers. Weber is a fine teacher with good administrative skills and a creative ability in envisioning the future. Having grown up in the Lutheran Church, he is now committed to The United Methodist Church and is able to keep the Kent Island United Methodists close to their Wesleyan heritage. Ball's relational skills and training in Christian education are tremendous benefits for the Sunday school, the UMYF, the confirmation class, and the Stephen's ministry. The staff, which also includes a full-time church secretary, part-time organist, choir director, and custodian, seemed to reflect cooperation and caring. Even so, a church of 1,200 could never run so smoothly with such a small staff without a great group of committed volunteers.

If the Kent Island church can maintain its current strengths, enlarge its financial base, continue to enlarge the spirit of cooperation between laity and staff, and dream God's dreams for its future, its roots and fruits will be as strong as the giant oak tree, which stands at its front door and whose beginning dates back to Bishop Francis Asbury's visit in 1774.

ST. JOHN'S UNITED METHODIST CHURCH

HAZLET, NEW JERSEY

John Johnson, Senior Pastor

What would you do if as a young newlywed pastor you were appointed to a 160-year-old church that had an average attendance of fewer than 30 members and was believed by conference officials to be dying? If your name were Norman Riley, you would stay 44 years and build it into the largest church in the conference with a membership of 2,400.

How did such a phenomenon occur? People within the church and within the community agree on several factors. The vitality of the church today is the lengthened shadow of the faith and energy of Riley. He had the ability to dream God's dream for the church and then to sell the dream.

A part of Riley's success was his ability to listen and to be flexible. For example, once a year at a Lenten Appreciation Dinner for all leaders and volunteer workers, Riley gave a "State of the Church" address. In it he listed his goals for the church for the coming year, which were written on newsprint. Then he invited the leaders to add their goals for the year. The one rule in the meeting was that no one could criticize another person's goal. The list was put into succinct form, and it became the purpose statement to be read at the meetings of the administrative board, United Methodist Women, and United Methodist Men. Goals achieved were marked through, and those not achieved were carried over to the next year or eliminated by the entire corps of leadership at the next appreciation dinner. Members felt they had a voice in the direction the church was going.

Perhaps equally as significant as Riley's ability to sell his dream was the fact that he, his wife, and their six children modeled the faith that was preached. The Rileys' two sons and four daughters, their spouses, and their children were and are still involved in every facet of ministry. This involvement is a highly visible example of the results of faith at work in the lives of individuals and of a long, successful pastorate.

Circumstances also account for a part of the church's growth. In 1960, a fire burned the small church building in which the congregation was worshiping. Fortunately they had been visionary enough to have bought four acres directly across the street. Now an attractive contemporary complex has been erected. Their sanctuary seats 800 persons. The church has two educational wings, a parsonage, and a gym and fellowship hall. In effect, the fire was a blessing in disguise, which allowed immediate expansion and greater visibility.

Another event that provided opportunity for growth occurred in 1952 when the Garden State Parkway was built. The Hazlet area numbered 8,000 then, but in 1989 the population was 30,000. Obviously, population growth does not necessarily mean church growth. There are other United Methodist churches in the area that have not grown. Members at St. John's intentionally reached out to the new residents by direct mail and house survey visits. These were friendly, "on the front steps" visits where members delivered a packet of materials in which facts about the community and the names and addresses of all churches in the community were listed. The packet also included program information about St. John's Church. Despite the fact that 85 percent of the new residents are Roman Catholic, the visits have created good will for the church and have resulted in a number of new members.

Churches that become known for specific well-done programs establish a good reputation for themselves. In 1959, the church members decided to have an outdoor crèche with live animals and real people at Christmastime. Through the years, the people have been replaced by life-size mannequins, but the animals continue to be live. The crèche was so well received that other things were gradually added, which include a large wall hanging in the form of a star containing needlepoint symbols of the Christian faith; a Chrismon tree; a Jesse tree; a St. Nicholas room; a 16-foot star in the sanctuary, containing live poinsettias; an Advent wreath; a live Christmas tree where choir members stood and sang; a large model of the Jerusalem Temple in Jesus' day, and a *Putz*. The *Putz* (German word for decoration) is a scale model of the Holy Land with water running through the streams and seas. Lights come on at the appropriate time to mark the narration of the journey of Mary and Joseph from Nazareth to Bethlehem. The *Putz* is used in connection with a 45-minute sound and light show, which tells the Christmas story. Each year during Advent, between 8,000 and 13,000 visitors come to see these displays. St. John's is known in the area as "the Christmas church."

The church is also known for the three apartment buildings for older adults which they have constructed on land immediately across the street from the church. The buildings contain 471 apartments. Government money was used for the construction, and the apartments are well built. They are operated by a separate corporate body composed of members of the church, and they are completely self-supporting. They were built not as a means of attracting new members (only 10 percent of the residents are now members of the church) but as a social outreach to older adults in the community. Church buses or vans are used as needed by the residents for doctor's appointments, grocery shopping, and other errands. Also, residents who are hospitalized are visited by the church staff.

Another reason for the church's growth is that there seems to be no power struggle within the membership. Rather, there is a family feeling. Though differences of opinion exist among the members, there is great unanimity in appreciation and support of the church. This feeling is cultivated through such activities as numerous family beach parties and dinners at the church.

In mid-1989, the senior pastor of 44 years retired. The transition to a new pastor has been smooth. The current pastor, Jack Johnson, has a good track record in former pastorates. In the Tom's River Church he also served as mayor of the town. He has excellent preaching and relational skills and will continue the period of solid growth for the congregation, as he brings his creative ideas and builds upon the solid foundation laid by Riley and members of St. John's Church.

SOUTHEASTERN JURISDICTION

FRAZER MEMORIAL UNITED METHODIST CHURCH

MONTGOMERY, ALABAMA

John Ed Mathison, Senior Pastor

Visiting Frazer Memorial United Methodist Church in Montgomery, Alabama, is like visiting first-century Christians. These people are "alive" Christians—loving, laughing, caring witnesses for Jesus Christ. The excitement evident among the members is contagious to persons attending Sunday morning worship in this fastest growing United Methodist church in America.

The people, factors, and circumstances that have come together to make this happen read like a novel. As in the Book of Acts, the central character in the Frazer story is Christ. Christ is lifted up in preaching, in music, in education, in giving, and in service. The chief apostle in this intriguing drama is John Ed Mathison, a low-key yet energetic man interested in athletics. He is, in fact, Montgomery's racquetball champion and holds Alabama's number one ranking for seniors in tennis.

Like Paul of the first century, this twentieth century apostle has a brilliant mind. He has a number of degrees: a B.A. from Huntington College; a B.D. from Candler School of Theology; a Th.M. in counseling from Princeton University; and a D.Min. in church growth from Candler School of Theology. He has the rare ability to perceive the sociological trends and spiritual needs in twentieth-century America and to build a church program that will meet those needs.

He took notice of the baby boomers and the protesters of the '60s who were looking for new meaning in their lives. Noting that these people were not looking at the denominational sign on the lawn, Mathison realized that they were seeking acceptance, warmth, and a philosophy that could withstand trying times. They were turned off by pontificating pastors and funereal music. Understanding their mood, Mathison encouraged his leaders to build high-demand ministries on meaning (commitment to Christ, service, tithing); warmth (accepting people where they are and helping them to experience God's love); growth (Bible study, Sunday school, and informal and spiritual growth groups and service projects); and lively worship. Mathison does not wear a robe. His 22-minute sermon is biblically based, outlined in the bulletin, and oriented toward everyday living. The music is varied and always lively.

Mathison models what he wants the church to be. His biggest job, as he sees it, is to choose staff wisely. He looks for Christian commitment, "people" skills, and vision in his staff. He reasons that job skills can be learned. He believes in long tenure for his staff and works to promote a sense of family.

Every day at 10:00 A.M., staff members have coffee together, and once a month they eat lunch together at a restaurant. Each Monday before coffee, they meet in the chapel to pray for staff concerns. Mathison encourages all staff persons to "run" their ministries, although he expects to be kept abreast of what is happening. He often tells the congregation, "We do not hire staff to do ministry, but to train you to do ministry. We are all ministers, and we should be out every day winning people for Christ."

Mathison encourages his staff to be active in the community. "That's where the unchurched are," he reminds them. Again, he is a model for the church staff through his own civic activities. He is highly visible through his weekly telecasts, both in the Alabama area and—through ACTS, the Baptist television network—in all of the states, including Hawaii and Alaska. He does daily radio devotionals and weekly devotionals for employees of several large corporations in Montgomery. Mathison believes that pastors should not spend too much time behind the desk. Despite his busy schedule, he gives persons meeting with him his undivided attention.

As important as the senior pastor's leadership and relational skills are to the success of this church, the secret of Frazer's success lies in the massive involvement of the laity. Each year, in a stewardship campaign called "In His Steps," the more than 5,000 members of the church are visited and given pledge cards with space for financial pledges and pledges to serve. As a result, amazing human and financial resources are made available to the church. In 1987, for example, in addition to a $3 million budget, Frazer members decreased their building debt significantly while building and paying for another new building. More important, 82 percent of the members are serving in some area of the church. Members have a strong sense of ownership.

Of course, none of the success could have been possible without the faithful group of disciples who made up the original Frazer Memorial Church, located in the central city. The congregation of about 400 members consisted mostly of blue-collar workers; only six in the membership had college degrees.

In the late '60s, the church learned that an interstate highway would be coming through the church's property. Because none of the members then lived in the neighborhood, the district superintendent recommended that they close the church and join another United Methodist church in Montgomery. The pastor, Walter Ellisor, and the members spoke as one voice—they would not close the church. Therefore the district board of church extension agreed to locate the church on the south side of town. The members were elated. Many people lived on the south side, so the church would have an opportunity to grow. They even bought a parsonage and moved the pastor in.

At the last minute, the district committee decided to give this south-side property to another church, but offered to buy five acres of land on the underdeveloped east side. The members at Frazer were discouraged. The property offered to them was a cotton patch, around which nobody lived. The land was 10 miles from the parsonage; the closest member lived four miles away. Only when they acknowledged their pioneer spirit and their determined faithfulness to be what they believed God wanted were the members of Frazer enabled to overcome their discouragement. The church did not lose a single member in the move.

In faith, they built a small chapel and a small education building. These remain today, along with six other buildings on an additional 20 acres on the heavily traveled Atlanta highway in one of the fastest growing areas of the city. God seemed to have a hand in this project from the beginning. The early members moved into the new sanctuary in 1970; the church had already grown to 551. In 1988 Frazer had more than 5,300 members with an average attendance of more than 3,300 in worship (the largest in United Methodism) and over 2,100 average attendance in Sunday school (the largest in United Methodism).

Sunday at the church includes breakfast at 7:30 A.M., three morning worship services, three Sunday schools, children's church at 9:40 A.M., and an evening worship service with an average attendance of 700. On Sunday afternoon, there is a program for children, UMYF and choir for youth, college fellowship, discipleship training, and rehearsals for 11 of the 37 choirs and instrumental groups. Other rehearsals follow or precede the large Wednesday evening fellowship dinner and Bible study. During the week, about as many programs and ministries are going on as there are people. Frazer United Methodist Church is an exciting place.

A number of United Methodist churches are growing today, but few are following the Great Commission to "make disciples" as effectively as is Frazer Memorial United Methodist Church.

BEN HILL UNITED METHODIST CHURCH

ATLANTA, GEORGIA

Walter Kimbrough, Senior Pastor

Since 1968, hundreds of neighborhoods, schools, and churches have gone through racial transition. In some cases, the transition has been smooth and all groups have benefited. In other situations, there have been misunderstandings and conflict. Some schools and churches have been sold or closed.

Fortunately for The United Methodist Church, the Ben Hill Church in Atlanta, Georgia, is much stronger than it was when the Civil Rights Bill was enacted. A log house was the first meeting place for the all-white church named Wesley Chapel, which was located in the Niskey Lake area of Atlanta. When demographic studies showed a shift in the population of the Ben Hill area of southwest Atlanta, the congregation voted in 1928 to move, to change its name to Ben Hill Methodist, and to build a new facility.

In the late '60s, when the neighborhood changed again and black people moved into the area, there was "white flight." Many people predicted that Ben Hill would close. Thanks to the small group of white people who remained—especially the pastor, Paul Wohlgemoth—the church stabilized in membership and began to grow slowly. Wohlgemoth or "Brother Paul," as he was affectionately known, made a personal call on each black family that visited the church. When a leadership position was open, Wohlgemoth very wisely filled it with a competent black person. Thus, as more white people left the area and more black people moved in, many black people joined the neighborhood church—Ben Hill.

In 1974 when Wohlgemoth completed his years of ministry at Ben Hill, the congregation asked for and received a black pastor, Cornelius Henderson. He was visionary and motivational, and the church began to grow. On his arrival, there were 300 members; average attendance was between 75 and 100. When he left in June 1986, the membership had grown to 4,300.

The membership as of October 1988 exceeded 5,600. Without exception, when we asked the lay people for their vision of the church in five years, they said, "At least 10,000 members." They feel especially blessed to have the present pastoral leadership of Walter Kimbrough. He is accelerating the rapid growth, increasing the involvement of the laity, strengthening the Sunday school, enlarging the number of weekday study groups, adding a fourth Sunday morning worship service (Ben Hill has three morning services and one in the evening), and broadening the outreach ministries. Staff and laity alike describe Kimbrough as outgoing in personality, dynamic in preaching and teaching, and a good organizer.

In outreach, the church has myriad activities: a food pantry, a blood bank, a counseling ministry, and work with the homeless. Ben Hill has adopted the Kimberly Court housing project to work with children and youth. The church has a satellite Sunday school there and works closely with the West Atlanta Elementary School, which the children in the project attend. The church has a pilot program with the Atlanta Hawks, whereby these athletes come to the school to speak about self-esteem, discipline, motivation, and the Christian faith. The Hawks also provide game tickets for the children, and the church provides transportation.

One of Ben Hill's finest outreach programs is its Preschool Academy for 110 children. Children, ages two through kindergarten, attend for the entire day. Other children come for after-school care. Each lead teacher must have a college degree, and the director is qualified academically, professionally, and personally. It is not surprising that the academy has a waiting list of two years.

Two other outstanding facets of Ben Hill's ministry include a well-trained staff and an excellent music program. The staff includes three ordained ministers. In addition to the senior pastor, there is a minister of visitation (a graduate of Gammon) and a young man (graduate of Lambuth

College and Duke Divinity School) who has supervision of the staff, youth ministry, and the recruitment of new members. The young woman who has the responsibility for children's ministries has an M.Div. degree. Pastoral care, counseling, and the singles' ministry are handled by a man with a doctoral degree. A seminary student at Gammon has responsibility for missions, and a young woman who is completing work for the diaconal ministry has responsibility for young adult work.

The director of administrative services, a Clark College graduate with a master's degree in educational administration, supervises the staff, which consists of an administrative secretary, a church secretary, one part-time secretary, a receptionist, a bookkeeper, a computer operator, a security staff of three, and a maintenance staff of five.

The music ministry has hundreds of participants. The sanctuary choir, for example, has 75 members; the youth choir has 140 members; and 150 persons make up the "Majestic Choir," a popular group that sings contemporary gospel music. In addition, the church has children's choirs, a men's chorus, a women's ensemble, and an orchestra. The choirs rotate for the three morning worship services, with additional special music from one of the smaller groups. Many persons are drawn to the church because of its dynamic worship.

Ben Hill members place strong emphasis on tithing. In fact, tithers bring their "tithes and offerings" to the altar each Sunday morning. Afterward, offering plates are passed to nontithers and visitors. Financial pledges are not taken from members; however, the church has so many tithers that the finances are in good shape.

Ben Hill is a great church. If it fulfills the pastor's dreams of strengthening the Sunday school, having more lay involvement, and building a larger sanctuary and family-life center, it will be even greater. Ben Hill should have no problem reaching the laity's goal of 10,000 active members.

ROSWELL UNITED METHODIST CHURCH

ROSWELL, GEORGIA

Malone Dodson, Senior Pastor

Roswell United Methodist Church, near Atlanta, Georgia, is a church that puts great emphasis upon prayer and the "warmth of a hug." One of the staff members said that his mother, a widow living out of the city, looks forward to her annual visit to the church because she says, "It's the only time I get hugged."

This permeating feeling of warmth and Christian love is no accident. The motto of the church is "We Care." In fact, Roswell's stated purpose is to help, encourage, and love people in the spirit of Jesus Christ. The church participates fully with the North Fulton Community Charities, maintains an on-site food pantry, and extends care to church members and people in the community.

The demographics of Roswell, Georgia, began to change in the early 1980s, moving from a population of 5,000 in 1980 to 50,000 in 1988. Demographers project that by 1992, Roswell will have 78,000 residents. Fortunately, the appointment of Malone Dodson to Roswell Church in June 1977 coincided with the city's growth.

The church grew from one Sunday morning worship service and one Sunday school in 1977 to three morning worship services and three Sunday schools in 1988. The staff consists of 35 persons, including six ordained clergy. Membership stands at 5,202, and the average worship attendance is 2,210.

Under the leadership of Dodson, special emphasis was placed on growth planning with thorough attention to details. The services of church consultant Ken Callahan of Dallas were used to help instigate and motivate the expansive building program that was necessary to continue ministry.

Roswell's balanced programming offers something for everyone. Lively worship sets the tone, with music that ranges from classical to contemporary, inspirational preaching, and the reading of prayer requests. Prayer is an important focus of the church, which is evident in their many prayer groups and forty-six neighborhood care groups. Each week, videotapes of the morning worship service are delivered to homebound members, and some videocassette recorders are provided where needed.

Fellowship, as well as prayer, is stressed because many members don't see one another during the week. Coffee and fellowship time takes place in 17 Sunday school classes each Sunday morning. Large Wednesday evening dinners provide fellowship and excellent programs.

Since the average age of the congregation is 42, Roswell has focused attention on ministry to children and youth. A weekday preschool program has an enrollment of 125. In addition to a strong Sunday school program, children may participate in any of six children's choirs and in children's worship study. Vacation Bible school will involve more than 600 children. A summer musical experience also is offered for young children. The congregation is invited to the final musical production.

Approximately 130 teenagers from 17 different high schools and 21 middle schools come to the church on Sunday evening for recreation, a snack supper, graded study, and worship. Retreats are offered in the spring and fall for middle and high school students, and a weekend confirmation retreat takes place each fall.

The singles ministry includes a yearly conference, and numerous support groups are especially geared to the needs of persons who are recently divorced, living in stepfamilies, widowed helping others, and varying other small support groups. Especially effective is the program "Rainbows for All God's Children," which is designed to assist children in small group settings. A monthly newsletter is published covering the activities of the singles and stepfamilies ministry. This ministry is staffed by a full-time pastor and director who meet the needs of young professionals, single parents, blended families, widowed persons, and "keenagers."

A counseling center is housed in a recently expanded facility. The counselors are part of the pastoral care of the church. They make hospital visits, participate in worship, lead workshops, and do personal counseling. In 1980, the ministry began with one part-time counselor. Today, three full-time counselors, four part-time counselors, and two support persons staff the center.

An excellent music program helps draw people to the church. In addition to the 209-voice sanctuary choir, there are two youth choirs, six children's choirs, handbell choirs, a children's handbell choir, and an orchestra. Twice a year, musical productions presented for two nights draw a large crowd. The Christmas concerts in 1989 drew about 5,000 listeners.

On March 19, 1989, Palm Sunday, the church occupied its new facility, which includes well-planned educational spaces, music practice, and office space, well-designed sacristy, proper facility for a weekday kindergarten with an enrollment of around 125, plus a beautiful 12-sided sanctuary that seats 2,000 and will include 26 memorialized stained glass windows and a large ceiling dome stained glass treatment. This now allows the congregation to worship and attend Sunday school at two worship times rather than the three previously needed.

Roswell United Methodist Church is alive and well. Ministry continues to expand as greater opportunities for continued service are recognized and met.

NORCROSS UNITED METHODIST CHURCH

NORCROSS, GEORGIA

Sam Coker, Senior Pastor

Like the children of Israel who claimed the Promised Land for God, so in 1987, members of Norcross United Methodist Church, Norcross, Georgia, stood in a chalk-drawn outline of a new 2,000-seat sanctuary and claimed it for the worship of God. One year later, on Easter Sunday, 1988, 3,015 persons worshiped for the first time in that beautiful sanctuary and consecrated it to the glory of God. An additional 400 persons could not get inside. How did such a miracle occur?

Actually, the miracle began in 1818 when some deeply committed Christians organized and later built Medlock Chapel in Gwinnett County. It soon became evident that two attributes characterized, and continue to characterize, this membership: commitment and vision. Their second church building was a white frame structure in the small town of Norcross.

In the early 1960s, before most people recognized the explosive growth that would come in Gwinnett County, members of Norcross Church bought nine and one-half acres on Beaver Ruin Road, one of the most heavily traveled areas of the county. This was a leap of faith and evidenced great vision on the part of the small membership church.

In 1968 the membership, numbering 600, built a fellowship hall/sanctuary and education space on their new property. Good location, explosive growth of the county, good pastoral leadership, and a committed, visionary membership enabled the church to grow from a membership of 1,455 in 1980 to 2,356 in 1985. In June 1989 the membership was 3,215, and for the last year the average worship attendance was 1,300, with a Sunday school average attendance of 927.

Their goal by the year 2,000 is 6,000 members and 4,000 in attendance each Sunday.

Despite limited facilities, the church was able to grow because of multiple use of space. In January 1982, the work area on education, after a year of careful study and preparation, implemented the plan for two Sunday school sessions and two worship services at Norcross. Growth occurred immediately. In July 1985, Sam Coker was appointed senior pastor. Attendance at worship celebrations continued to grow, but there wasn't room; hence the erection of the 2,000-seat sanctuary in 1988.

Coker seems to be the "right man at the right place at the right time." He is a man of unusual preaching ability. In addition, his high energy level seems to match the dynamic growth pattern of the county in which the church is located.

Many new members join Norcross United Methodist Church because of "Sam's preaching" or the worship celebration—and a celebration it is! Each service is alive with an air of spontaneity and excitement.

Often, appropriate music is placed in the celebration without including it in the printed order. The members are encouraged to bring their Bibles to the worship celebrations. When the scripture lesson is read, the congregation stands and follows the reading in their Bibles. The congregation also follows the reading of scriptural references during the sermon.

A great variety of music is used to appeal to the wide age range and musical tastes of the congregation. The focal point of the celebration is the sermon. Coker is a biblical preacher who relates the Word of God to the personal and collective needs of the congregation. He moves from behind the pulpit to be closer to his people, and he speaks with a sense of urgency flavored with humor. The people experience a great feeling of warmth, freedom, and closeness to Christ and to each other. It is not surprising that most of the 400 persons who join the church each year come through this joyous worship service.

Other strengths of the church include a large Sunday school with quality educational opportunities for children, youth, and adults; an excellent staff, which receives respect and appreciation from the large congregation and obviously enjoys a sense of camaraderie among themselves; excellent preschool and mother's day out programs; and balanced programming for all age groups, including a large singles' ministry and a creative program for older adults.

Coker sees himself as "coach" of this very large team of players—both staff and laity. He believes that one of his most significant tasks is choosing the right persons for staff positions. His criteria include their having a personal relationship with Jesus Christ and feeling "called" into ministry. They also must be self-starters, take coaching well, and be willing to grow. Staff members must be able to motivate volunteers and to delegate authority, be willing to support the church financially, and be high energy people.

Among the number of distinctive ministries in this lively, thriving church is one for couples who plan to be married. Concerned about the continuing number of failed marriages in the United States, and convinced that faith is the cornerstone of a happy marriage, pastors require that a couple be members of the church and attend worship at least six months before they are married. By this time a pattern of regular worship has been established, and they have been assimilated into the life of the church.

A part of the assimilation is attending premarital classes including such subjects as "Expectations in Marriage," "Finances," "Communication," and "Sexuality." They also see and discuss the video "Before You Say I Do" by Tim and Beverly LaHaye. Because the church averages two weddings a week, it is easy to form new Sunday school classes from the premarital counseling classes.

For new parents, a volunteer will make a call in the home. She explains nursery care at the church, talks about baptism, and presents a scrapbook, which includes news clippings of outstanding world events that occurred on the day of the baby's birth. The volunteer also presents the rosebud that was on the altar in recognition of the child's birth.

Each fall, all the ministries of the church, from educational ministries, fix-it, performing arts, foreign missions, "Continuing Christmas" (emergency aid to the needy), to the music ministry are offered to the congregation through the campaign titled "Yes, Lord!" Each member is asked to prayerfully commit to his or her place of service in and through the church. This is prioritized (1, 2, 3, 4, and 5). Within a short time, every member is contacted and informed as to when he or she will begin to serve.

Sunday evening services include a snack supper for all ages. While children and youth meet separately, the adults meet together to study subjects of current interest, such as "The New Age" philosophy. The services are held in the chapel to a "standing room only" congregation. Interspersed among the studies are traditional evening worship celebration services.

On New Year's Eve there is a burning service. Members write on a card anything they wish to leave behind before entering the new year, such as habits, grief, or negative attitudes. The cards are brought to the altar and placed in a clay urn in which a lighted candle has been placed in wet sand.

Norcross is a good example of the "church being the church." It is introducing people to Jesus Christ, seeking to make them true disciples, and sending them forth as ministers and evangelists. If the growth of Norcross United Methodist Church continues and if its assimilation program matches its recruitment, there is no reason why their dream for the year 2000—6,000 members with an average attendance of 4,000—cannot be realized.

LAKE MAGDALENE UNITED METHODIST CHURCH

TAMPA, FLORIDA

Brad Dinsmore, Senior Pastor

One Sunday in November, 1989, Lake Magdalene United Methodist Church celebrated a "Thanksgiving Harvest of New Members" when 131 persons joined the church. These were people who had visited the church over several months—even years in some cases, and for one reason or another had not made a decision to join. They were invited to an orientation dinner followed by a question and answer period concerning the Christian faith and the ministries of Lake Magdalene Church. At that time they were given an opportunity to indicate whether or not they wished to join. Ninety-nine percent of those present chose to join at the Thanksgiving Harvest of New Members service.

Though more than the usual number of persons came into the membership that day, the service was symbolic of the growth and creativity evident in this exciting church. In 1980, the membership was 1,138, and today it stands at 2,600. How did this happen during a time when many United Methodist churches, even in this same geographic area, were declining?

A part of the answer has to do with demographics. The suburban area of Lake Magdalene grew by 4 percent during eight of those years. Yet, the annual church growth of 11 percent far outdistanced the population growth. The church leaders agree that the major reason was the arrival of Brad Dinsmore as senior pastor in 1980. In addition to being a superb communicator and having good relational and communicative skills, Dinsmore's unique talent, according to the leaders, is the ability to motivate and empower laity. As one said: "He is not only a visionary who can sell his dream, but he also enables us to dream big dreams and then empowers us to implement those dreams." And dream they have!

From the beginning in 1895, when a small Evangelical United Brethren congregation was organized in the Lake Magdalene area, church members have been characterized as having spiritual depth, an interest in Christian education, and an ability to dream God's dream. Those attributes still characterize this vital congregation.

"The major difference during the past ten years is that Brad has helped us look beyond ourselves for ministry," one of the church leaders told us. She explained that in 1980 they had plans to erect a building which would contain, among other things, an up-to-date kitchen and fellowship hall for large dinners for their mainly "over-50" congregation. When Dinsmore arrived, he suggested that before they built, they might want to do a demographic study of their community. To their amazement they learned that instead of finding "empty nesters" (couples whose children had grown up and left home) moving into the five-mile area surrounding the church, there was an influx of baby boomers (young adults born between 1946 and 1964).

Today 47.7 percent of the membership are between the ages of 26 and 45. In addition to Heritage Hall, their facilities include an educational building, a four-story life enrichment center, and a sanctuary, which is the oldest of their buildings. The master plan includes the erection of a new sanctuary. These buildings are on an eight-acre corner lot on a heavily trafficked thoroughfare. Fortunately, the church has the first option to buy another eight acres adjoining their property.

Though their buildings are impressive, this is not a church with an "edifice complex." The facilities are simply a means to ministry in this seven-day-a-week congregation.

The purpose of all these ministries is graphically depicted in the missional statement, which is carried in every church brochure and given to each new member. The statement reads:

1. To so present Christ by the power of the Holy Spirit that persons come to know God through him; accept

him as Savior; and serve him as Lord through the church.

2. To identify, lead, incorporate, and equip persons in becoming disciple-makers.
3. To affirm, nurture, and assist persons in becoming what God intended them to be.
4. To engage in the ministry of reconciliation of body, and spirit through loving missional outreach.

Their theme, "Offering a place, a purpose, and The Person," is well known by the members.

The focal point of the church is worship. According to the survey taken in orientation classes, more people come into the church through worship than through any other port of entry. On Sunday morning the three services of worship are at 8:30, 9:45, and 10:55. The services are traditional but informal. A strong emphasis is placed on warmth and friendliness, with a specified time in the order of worship for greeting each other and visitors in the congregation. There is a minimum of liturgy and a variety of music, but "more Gaither than Bach." The senior pastor wears a robe but stands away from the pulpit in the chancel area and uses no notes. His sermons are biblically based but related to twentieth-century living and more specifically to the needs of his parishioners. He is not a lectionary preacher.

The second most important channel of membership is Christian education where the average attendance in Sunday school is 628. Special emphasis has been given to new classes for young adults with a resultant emphasis on quality learning for children and youth.

The reputation of having a superior preschool program helps new families in the community know about the church. A child-care program exists for one- and two-year-olds, and preschool for three-year-olds through kindergarten. Three hundred children are currently enrolled, and there is always a waiting list.

In the youth program, a diaconal minister works, not just with young people, but with their families as well. One of her goals is working toward Christian family lifestyles. In addition to Sunday school, a Sunday evening program for junior and senior highs includes recreation, singing, a message by the youth minister, and small group discussion.

A unique "Friday Night Alive" program is conducted for eighth and ninth graders. The program is held in Heritage Hall and is open to all young people in this age group in the community. The attendance each Friday evening is between 200 and 300. Food, contemporary music (screened by a committee including the youth minister), dancing, and many adults are found at Friday Night Alive. Another plus for the youth program are the 26 Scout troops that meet— including Cubs, Girl Scouts, and Boy Scouts.

A good blending of ministries nurtures the members and offers a bold outreach to others. During the past ten years, mission giving has gone from $22,000 to $165,000. Other outreach programs include an annual mission fair, mission trips, and participation in metropolitan ministries.

Other evidences of balanced programming are the Bible study groups, which meet Wednesday and Thursday evenings, Stephen's ministry, singles' ministry, strong and active units of United Methodist Women and United Methodist Men, and an emphasis upon family ministries.

One of the obvious strengths of this church is a highly qualified staff which works harmoniously with each other and with laity. If Lake Magdalene United Methodist Church can continue to emphasize celebrative worship, quality Christian education, strong fellowship, and missional outreach, and if the church can continue to dream God's dream and have the courage to implement the dream, they will become a metropolitan church of 4,500 members, as projected, by the year 2000.

NORTH CENTRAL JURISDICTION

SAINT LUKE'S UNITED METHODIST CHURCH

INDIANAPOLIS, INDIANA

E. Carver McGriff, Senior Pastor

On 14 acres in an affluent, suburban section of Indianapolis is St. Luke's United Methodist Church, the fastest growing church in the North Central Jurisdiction. In its 33-year history, the church has grown to its present membership of 4,166 persons, with a Sunday worship averaging more than 1,800 adults. Much of that growth has come during the 23-year tenure of the popular current senior pastor, E. Carver McGriff.

McGriff is an excellent communicator. Having had a career in business before he entered the ministry, he understands the secular world and speaks in "non-churchy" language. His 18- to 20-minute sermons present the gospel message in a succinct, contemporary, and persuasive manner. He speaks without notes and in a conversational tone. It is not surprising that when we asked the question, "Why do so many people join this church?" the unanimous response from the laity and staff alike was "Carver's preaching."

McGriff's appeal is to all age groups, but young professionals, many of whom have never joined a church, have responded most readily. As a result, each year more adults join St. Luke's on profession of faith than by transfer of membership from other United Methodist churches or from other denominations. During the last 10 years, hundreds have come into the membership by profession of faith.

Actually the church's follow-up on first-time visitors reflects McGriff's philosophy for winning persons for Christ and church membership. He uses the imagery of iron filings laying on a table. Instead of picking up each one separately, he believes all of them can be picked up at once by using a magnet. For church membership he is convinced that the magnet is a carefully timed, unritualistic, and fully alive worship service.

Three such services are held at 8:30, 9:30, and 11:00 A.M. each Sunday. The music director-organist, who is especially sensitive to the flow of the service, sees to it that there are no dead places in the services. In addition, the special music in each service appeals to a variety of musical tastes—from classical to gospel to contemporary—and is presented by one of the many choirs, ensembles, soloists, or instrumentalists.

Though there is a follow-up letter to visitors after their first visit, no further contacts are made until their third visit. At that time, they are invited to attend a four-week membership class (held on Sunday afternoons), and their names are put into the computer to receive the congregation's newsletter and other church mailings. Attendance at membership classes is required if one wishes to join.

The variety of music, the persuasiveness of the preaching, and the simplicity of the service (which consists of two uplifting hymns, no responsive reading, and the creed and scriptures printed in the bulletin) all make it easy for everyone to feel at home. Incidentally, a family-oriented worship experience, including a children's sermon, is conducted by one of the associate pastors at 7:00 P.M. each Sunday. If members attend and join because of worship, they stay and become active because of the excellent programming. The four-page bulletin insert listing "Opportunities for the Week" looks as inclusive as an airline flight schedule. There is something for everyone, from Bible and book studies to crafts, exercise, and meetings of Overeaters Anonymous. On the Sunday we visited, we discovered that 300 meetings were scheduled in a one-month period.

Such a varied offering is made possible by a competent staff, including six ordained clergy (two of whom are women). The women clergy not only are accepted but are warmly affirmed by the congregation.

Despite the fact that the stability of a long-tenured staff had been temporarily shaken by some clergy divorces and unexpected moves, there is still a strong feeling of cooperative collegiality. This spirit is modeled by the senior pastor who chose no preferential treatment in the allocation of office space, but, along with other clergy, drew out of a hat his assigned office. Though he exerts great care in selection of staff, McGriff has a *laissez-faire* leadership style, which not only motivates these self-starters on the staff, but also tends to release their creative powers as well.

In addition to worship, opportunities for fellowship and study mold this well-educated congregation of upwardly mobile professionals (average age 35 to 40) into a caring Christian community. Their very fine study program at Sunday school is enhanced throughout the week by small group studies and elective seminars from time to time. Also, members have an opportunity for weekly fellowship at coffee hours, scheduled between the morning worship services and the two Sunday schools. These gatherings are not just superficial "small talk" fellowships, but show authentic caring made possible through neighborhood shepherding groups. Through this network of indepth caring, members share each other's joys and sorrows.

An example of the growing spirit of koinonia is seen in the enlarged attendance at the annual church picnic. The event is publicized only through the shepherding network. At the picnic, neighborhood groups sit together. The attendance has grown from 400 when it began nine years ago to 900 in September 1989.

As they look toward the future, members of this dynamic church want continued growth in attracting new members and in assimilating them fully into the Body of Christ at St. Luke's. They have an expressed desire to expand the support of missions. Their young people have participated in summer service projects, and adults have served on work teams in Nicaragua. Staff and lay leaders want to expand financial giving and service to missions.

Other targeted areas for continued growth include singles, children, youth, and family ministries. Though there are few older adult members, church leaders want to project a plan for this group as the congregation ages.

The big test for the stability of the church will come when McGriff retires. If the church can make this transition with a relative sense of ease, St. Luke's United Methodist Church will continue to grow.

MOUNT AUBURN UNITED METHODIST CHURCH

GREENWOOD, INDIANA

Nelson Chamberlin, Senior Pastor

What happens to a growing congregation when it experiences storms both internally and externally? Within four years, Mount Auburn United Methodist Church had a senior pastor who left the denomination and started an independent congregation in Florida; an associate pastor who started an independent church only two miles away, taking with him several hundred Mount Auburn members and their financial support; and in the middle of all this a tornado ripped through Greenwood, Indiana, almost completely destroying the church's sanctuary and part of the church's educational wing.

Any one of the above traumas could have decimated a less hardy congregation. The members at Mount Auburn, however, have not only survived but are showing signs of marvelous vitality. Just as a physical body experiences pain from trauma, the Body of Christ at Mount Auburn has suffered. Yet under the able leadership of Nelson Chamberlin, his staff, and a corps of dedicated laypersons, the wounds seem to be healing and the church is courageously facing forward.

Saint Paul told the Christians in Rome that "in everything, as we know, [God] cooperates for good with those who love God." And good things have come from Mount Auburn's pain. Instead of rebuilding the sanctuary, they rebuilt that structure as educational space, adding a second floor as a teen center for community use. The center has proved to be an excellent means of outreach. Open Thursday through Sunday evenings, as many as 150 youth attend Saturday evenings. The program is supervised by the Mount Auburn minister of youth and volunteer counselors from the church. Incidentally, the congregation now worships in an improvised fellowship hall. The sanctuary and a family life center are included in the church's long-range master plan.

The bottom floor of the former sanctuary building is now used for another ministry, a well-staffed preschool and day-care program. The preschool program is not new. In fact, on the day of the storm, 138 children were in the church building. Though there had been no warning of a tornado, the sky was dark and the director suddenly felt led to say, "Boys and girls, I believe that this is a good day for a pretend tornado drill." Therefore, when the twister took the roof off and tore down the walls, 138 children and their teachers were lying face down on the floor of the corridor. Miraculously, no one was seriously injured.

The preschool director was calmly creative rather than frantically frightened in a crisis. When the senior pastor came into the damaged building and saw "hot" electrical wires hanging down, and smelled gas from the broken gas main, he said to her, "We must evacuate the children immediately." Quick as a flash, she said enthusiastically, "Boys and girls, we are now going to have a parade in the rain." Thus, in a torrential downpour, she marched 138 children across the street to a building which housed the church offices. Surely God's hand was on Mount Auburn that day.

When Mount Auburn Church was organized in 1826, the area was a small rural community, and it remained that until the 1970s, when Indianapolis began to grow to the south. Today, Johnson County is the fourth fastest growing county in the state. Subdivisions now dot the landscape. Because of the good school system, many young families with children are moving into the area.

The older members of the congregation deserve much credit, for they have welcomed newcomers not only into church membership but into leadership roles as well. Today, the average age of the 935 members is approximately 45. A part of the 17 acres owned by the church has been made into playing fields and serves as a community athletic field. That, too, has become an important outreach to new people.

An innovative visitation approach to local persons who visit the church for the first time is now being used. All first-time visitors receive on the Monday after they attend church, a visit from a lay member of the congregation who brings a freshly baked pie. The pies are baked at the church on Monday afternoon and are delivered after 4:00 P.M. If no one is home, the boxed pie is left in a safe place with the following handwritten note: "A stranger is a friend we haven't met yet. Thank you for coming to Mount Auburn United Methodist Church." To date more than 70 percent of the pie-receiving visitors have returned to worship.

Another outreach ministry is to single persons. Though the community still consists mostly of two-parent families, there is a growing number of singles. In addition to a singles' program for all age groups led by the associate pastor, the senior pastor and his wife lead divorce recovery workshops at least twice a year.

The two worship services on Sunday morning with Sunday school in between are the focal point of the congregation. Chamberlin has insisted that his associate, Charles Berdel, preach every other Sunday. They preach at both services on their respective Sundays. This magnanimous spirit has permeated the staff and enhanced the development of a high sense of morale.

Music is a vital part of worship and outreach. Carol Koenig, the daughter and daughter-in-law of United Methodist pastors, has been director of music for several years. She leads nine choirs, including three handbell choirs. Two cantatas are presented each year, usually during Advent and in the spring. Koenig directs music for the summer daily vacation Bible school, at the end of which a children's musical is presented. She regularly leads music for the church's preschool program. Other members of the staff include a full-time preschool director, a full-time office manager, a part-time director of Christian education, a part-time business manager, a part-time secretary, and a resident counselor.

If this congregation can reduce its debt for the building, increase its concern for and giving to others, continue to avoid bitterness, and work together under the question, "What does God want this church to be?," then Mount Auburn Church will be like a lighthouse giving light and hope to other churches experiencing difficulties.

HYDE PARK COMMUNITY UNITED METHODIST CHURCH

CINCINNATI, OHIO

Douglas Mullins, Senior Pastor

"Now when I am on vacation I have no place to go," said Douglas Mullins, the senior pastor at Hyde Park Community Church in Cincinnati, Ohio. When asked for an explanation, he said that during his years of ministry in smaller churches, he had spent at least one of his vacation Sundays each year attending the large cathedral church of his conference. He knew he would experience great worship and excellent preaching there. He is now the senior pastor of that cathedral-type church, and according to members the quality of worship and preaching is still excellent.

The massive Gothic structure was built in 1929 after the merger of two smaller congregations. Even today, it is surprising to think that only 409 members would have had the vision and courage to erect such a magnificent building, which covers a city block and includes a large refectory; a beautiful parlor and library, both of which are paneled in warm oak and contain handsome English furniture; a community-sized theater for dramatic and musical productions; and a gymnasium.

Unfortunately the building was completed just before the Great Depression of the '30s, necessitating several years of financial struggle. The doors of the church were kept open thanks to several of the members who were willing to mortgage personal property; all gave sacrificially.

This forward-looking, visionary spirit seems to have characterized the church through the years. Though the city of Cincinnati has changed drastically through the years, the Hyde Park community has remained stable. It is a community of upper middle-class homes and attractive shops. Many upwardly mobile young adults have bought the handsome old homes, allowing the church to continue having young families. One of the church's most popular programs for community outreach is an excellent preschool and child-care center.

The most valued focus of the church, from the point of view of a cross-section of members, is vital worship, with special emphasis upon great preaching. The church has had great preachers throughout the years, perhaps the most notable of which is Emerson Colaw, who served the church for 19 years before his election to the episcopacy in 1980. Mullins, too, is recognized for his preaching ability.

According to the leaders, the morning worship experience is more high church than that of many United Methodist churches. The excellent chancel choir is conducted by a professor of music from the Cincinnati Conservatory of Music. The choir presents several major works each year, and every Sunday the anthems are classically traditional. Though a great appreciation is expressed for this, there are also several suggestions that the musical offerings be more varied, including some contemporary music to reach the young adults who are attending.

Other pluses for this congregation include good staff, excellent pastoral care—especially for older adults and homebound, and good ministries for children, youth, and singles. Both junior high and senior high groups have excellent programs and participation because of the superior lay leadership and staff support. An example of their ambitious planning is the summer European trip for youth, the money for which has been raised by the young people. In addition, they will have two summer work teams in Appalachia.

United Methodist Women at Hyde Park have stayed strong through their willingness to stay flexible. As more and more women join the work force, the general meetings for United Methodist Women have been set to meet varying schedules.

The future of this great congregation should continue to be bright. To a degree this will be determined by how well the strong, excellent ideas of the senior pastor are accepted and endorsed by staff and lay leaders.

CASTLETON UNITED METHODIST CHURCH

INDIANAPOLIS, INDIANA

Charles Armstrong, Senior Pastor

Churches, like people, have personalities. With both, the personality develops early in life. From the beginning, Castleton United Methodist Church in Indianapolis, Indiana, has had a core of laypersons who were committed, visionary risk takers.

Established in 1843, the church reflected the life and mores of the rural village of Castleton, located in the northeastern section of Indianapolis. In the late 1960s, the life of the church changed dramatically with the building of an interstate system and the completion of the Castleton mall. In fact, the junction of I-465 and I-69 was designed to be located on the site of the church property.

Church members had a decision to make. Would they build another small church building in that neighborhood or choose a larger site and build for growth, which according to demographic studies would most surely occur? The church was not united in this decision, but the majority—200 people—voted to be visionary and "lean into the future."

Fortunately for them, a dentist, who was a church member, owned a sizeable plot of land adjacent to his home. He offered to sell it at a very reasonable price to the church and to the Masonic Lodge whose property was also being taken by the interstate system. Thus, the church secured eight and one half acres on a corner of the heavily traveled North Shadeland Avenue. They immediately built a parsonage; soon thereafter, in 1967, they built a combination sanctuary/ education building. The congregation worshiped in that first building (now the fellowship hall) until Christmas Eve 1983, when they moved into their present sanctuary with 759 persons in attendance.

At the time the church moved from its earlier location, there were 469 members, one pastor, one secretary, an organist, and a choir director. Average attendance in Sunday school was 248 (100 of whom were children) and 313 in worship. Presently the membership is 1,622 and is growing at the rate of 15 percent per year. Average attendance in Sunday school is 357 with 325 of them being children, and a worship attendance of 562. The present church staff is composed of 13 persons, including four pastors, a counselor, a director of education and preschool program, a director of adult education, a secretary, an administrative secretary, a financial secretary, a director of music, an organist, a building supervisor, and a custodian.

If the present growth rate continues, the church will grow over the next 10 years to 2,300 members, with 850 people in worship and 780 in Sunday school, 500 of whom will be children.

What accounts for such growth? In addition to the obvious population growth in the community, the following factors seem significant: beautiful buildings with high visibility; gifted and visionary leadership—both staff and laity; an excellent preschool program which has a good reputation in the community; good balance between ministries of congregational care and outreach; and unity of spirit within the congregation.

As in most growing churches, Castleton United Methodist Church reflects the leadership and spirit of its senior pastor, Charles (Chuck) Armstrong. A gregarious, warm person, Armstrong, according to church leaders, is extremely relational, a fine preacher and a good administrator. As one leader described him, "He guides, not decides for laity." He also makes regular personal contacts through visits with members and prospective members. According to his own record, he averages 45 calls a month besides hospital calls. Leaders say that the senior pastor's wife is also a strength of the church. Her friendliness and hospitality and her involvement in the life of the church are seen as assets.

One of the reasons for growth is the thorough follow-up of visitors. Under the direction of the minister of discipleship, the plan includes lay visitation on Sunday afternoon. On

Monday, information gained about the visitor is typed on individual cards and filed. A letter goes from the senior pastor on Monday, and he makes a telephone call to each of the visitors later in the week. The following week, a visit is made by one of the associate pastors if such a visit is requested. When visitors return for worship or otherwise show an interest in the church, they are helped to find a small group in which they can participate.

The new member orientation classes are held bi-monthly on the first Sunday afternoon from 1:00 to 4:30. Everyone meets together for one hour and studies the meaning of membership and the history of United Methodism and of Castleton church. This single group also looks at the long-range plan of the church. Then, the large group is broken into three smaller groups to visit program learning centers of Christian education, music ministry, congregational care, and missions. After a refreshment break (provided by United Methodist Women), they come back together for an hour to fill out interest indicators for their study and volunteer service and pledge cards for their financial support.

The preschool program is an excellent port of entry for new members. The program was begun 22 years ago, and more than 200 families have joined the membership as a result. Today, 225 children are enrolled, and the staff consists of 17 qualified and certified teachers.

The minister to youth has created great excitement among young people, their parents, and church leaders. He believes that one of his real responsibilities is to train and equip leaders of youth. Twenty-four adult leaders, or one adult for every six young people, are active in the program. His dream is to have one adult for every three young people. In addition to Sunday school and United Methodist Youth Fellowship, the youth program includes confirmation classes, work camps, retreats, weekly Tuesday evening discussion groups, Friday morning (6:30) Bible study, peer counseling, newsletters, and parenting classes.

Quality Christian education for children, youth, and adults is provided in two Sunday school sessions, which meet concurrently with the worship services each Sunday morning at 9:30 and 10:45. In addition to Sunday school for children, a large vacation Bible school is conducted each summer. Two children's choirs and an adult choir perform regularly. In a church where the average age is 43, there is an active program for older adults called "Variety Bunch."

The carefully designed ministry of congregational care includes a shepherding program, Stephen's ministry, and "Dinners for Six." Congregational care is greatly enhanced by a resident counselor on the staff.

Castleton United Methodist Church is a thriving, exciting church where good things are happening. Their long-range plans include additional education space, a youth facility, redevelopment of the existing music department, addition of staff, and spiritual growth. In fact, they have met with an architect to see designs for a 16-room fellowship hall, youth center, and sanctuary expansion program. If the present membership proves to be as visionary as their predecessor, the future of this church is assured.

CHURCH OF THE MESSIAH UNITED METHODIST

WESTERVILLE, OHIO

Robert Ball, Senior Pastor

In Westerville, an affluent, suburban area of Columbus, Ohio, the United Methodist churches proclaim the Lordship of Jesus Christ in their names—Church of the Savior, Church of the Master, Church of the Messiah. Among them the Church of the Messiah was one of the five fastest growing churches of the North Central Jurisdiction from 1980 to 1985. Today it is on the rise again.

Located on State Street, just a few blocks from the distinctive shops and boutiques of Uptown Westerville and on the main thoroughfare off Interstate 270, the contemporary buildings of the church are visible. Organized in 1818, the church has literally grown up with the community. In the past 20 years, Westerville has grown in population from 5,000 to 30,000, and the explosive growth occurred from 1980 to 1985. The projected population growth of the community by the year 2000 is 50,000.

Other factors in the church's dramatic step forward included the transformational leadership of a visionary senior pastor, Larry Hard, whose warmth of personality and leadership skills enabled the members to catch his vision; an excellent music program; and a minister of education who strengthened the Sunday school and began a dynamic youth program.

As often happens in the life of a church when a popular pastor leaves, membership declined. A controversial building program, entailing the tearing down of an existing building, added to the loss. Today the future looks bright again. The building program is complete. The new educational facility greatly enhanced the appearance of existing buildings and enlarged the opportunities for new ministries.

Significantly, a senior pastor, whose talents and interests seem to fit the congregation, arrived in June 1989. Robert Ball is an outgoing, warm individual who is an excellent preacher and a good administrator. His collegial style of leadership is especially appreciated by the staff. Also a new churchwide spirit of enthusiasm and unity can serve as a powerful impetus for a forward thrust.

Perhaps the greatest port of entry for new members is congregational worship. The three Sunday morning services are at 8:30, 9:45, and 11:00. Coffee fellowship follows each of the worship services, and Sunday school sessions are held at 9:45 and 11:00 A.M. The worship services are traditional but warm with lively music and an opportunity for the expression of congregational concerns.

In a jurisdiction and conference where membership losses have been great, the Church of the Messiah stands out as a radiant example of what can happen when a congregation of caring people become intentional about being the people of God. Balanced programming for all age groups seems characteristic of this growing church. Especially significant ministries include Our Day (a preschool program); youth programs—including confirmation; music programs; and adult education.

Reaching the baby boomers is a goal of most United Methodist congregations, and the Church of the Messiah is achieving that goal. Excellent Christian education is one of the things baby boomers want for their children. At the Church of the Messiah, babies have Christian child care until they are one and a half. Then Christian learning experiences are begun. Special times of enrichment for all children are offered through "Super Saturdays" and vacation Bible school in the summer.

One of the ministries especially recognized throughout the community is their five-day-a-week preschool program. Parents are allowed to send their two- to four-year-old children two days a week. Currently 300 children are enrolled, and there is a waiting list.

Many parents join Messiah Church to allow their seventh grade children to participate in the nine-month confirmation classes, which are held from 4:00 to 5:30 P.M. on Sundays. In addition to classes on what it means to be a Christian, what it means to be a Protestant, and what it means to be a member of Church of the Messiah, the children go on field trips to churches of other denominations and attend a week-end retreat.

In order to allow the confirmand to feel a part of the entire congregation, each young person is assigned a confirmation friend who is an older member. They meet each other at a dinner given by parents of the confirmand. These confirmation friends stay in touch during the months of confirmation and stand in the congregation when "their" young person is confirmed. Last year 44 seventh graders were confirmed, and 40 are currently enrolled in the classes.

In addition to regular Sunday school classes designed for youth, 18 counselors are serving the youth on Sunday evening in the United Methodist Youth Fellowship. Four youth choirs, two choral and two bell choirs, involve young people. Youth choirs sing or ring twice a month at the 9:45 A.M. worship service. They present a musical at least once a year and go on a summer choir tour. Another group of Messiah youth participate in a mission work team in South Carolina. Also, members appreciate the human sexuality workshop for parents and youth, which is conducted annually.

Music is a vital part of the church's ministry. The director of music completed a master's degree in choral conducting at Ohio University in 1979. His professor, Mrs. Helen Swank, was choir director at Messiah at the time. When the church decided to hire a full-time director, Mrs. Swank urged Lindsay Smith to apply for the position. He was employed and has been there for 10 years. There are 14 choirs—eight choral groups and six bell choirs. In addition, instrumentalists play often in services of worship. Other musical events include major works performed twice each year by the chancel choir, a children's musical, an annual hymn sing, and a medieval Christmas feast, with music and food service by youth choir members. Smith emphasizes to all members of his choirs that theirs should never be just a performance, but "an opportunity to praise God and bring people to Christ."

Though many churches do not stress Christian education for adults, Messiah has over 300 adults involved in eight

Sunday school classes. There are also Bible studies on Wednesday mornings and Thursday evenings, a "moms support group" for mothers of small children, circles for United Methodist Women, and study groups on such topics as parenting, mental health, and infertility. These are done in conjunction with the Elizabeth Blackwell Center of Riverside Methodist Hospital of Columbus. Messiah older adults are alive and well. They have a month program meeting, luncheon, and trips to such places as England and the Caribbean.

Growth in the church doesn't just happen. It is carefully planned. For example, first-time visitors are contacted within the week and as often as possible on the day of their first visit. All first-time visitors receive a letter from the senior pastor and a phone call from a member of the congregation. After the second visit a personal call is made in the home by the Minister of Outreach. Great care is taken not to overwhelm them to the extent of seeming to be pushy. The church carefully monitors continued attendance or lack of attendance until the church can determine if the visitors are interested in becoming members. The Minister of Outreach, who has been with the church for 14 years, says that they yearly set a numerical goal for new members. This year the church expects to receive at least 200 persons.

If this growing church can continue to have celebrative worship, quality programming, and excellent staff; if they are willing to expand their ministries, enlarge their financial base, and be visionary about their future, there is no reason why Church of the Messiah United Methodist cannot become one of the great metropolitan churches of our denomination.

ANOKA UNITED METHODIST CHURCH

ANOKA, MINNESOTA

Gordon M. Wendland, Senior Pastor

Gordon Wendland is in his fourteenth year as senior pastor of the 135-year-old Anoka United Methodist Church, Anoka, Minnesota. Much of the church's growth has occurred during his ministry.

In 1968 the congregation left the original site in downtown Anoka and bought a five-acre plot in a rapidly growing residential area. Today there are 1,236 members. During these years, the congregation has built a well-equipped educational building with a spacious kitchen and a large fellowship hall, which served as a sanctuary for 16 years.

In addition to growing numerically under the leadership of Wendland, the members have paid off the debt on the educational unit and constructed a handsome 350-seat sanctuary of contemporary design. The chancel windows, made of faceted glass, tell the story of God's continuing creation. They and the additional side windows were designed by an active member of the congregation, who is a former professor of art.

As the members make plans for retiring the remaining debt on the sanctuary, they wisely are planning for the future with emphasis on meeting the expressed needs of people through new programming and additional staff. For example, to replace one full-time assistant pastor who left to assume her own pastorate, they have employed five part-time specialists. These include a young couple who work in Christian education. The wife works especially in children's ministries, and the husband with youth ministries. The new assistant pastor, while completing her seminary work, will also bring to the staff her counseling and organizational skills. There is a new chancel choir director and a new orchestra leader. Three laypersons from the congregation will direct the two children's choirs and the adult bell choir. The additional full-time staff includes a minister of visitation, a church secretary, and a custodian.

Excitement has mounted as the new program has come into place. In the past, Sunday school for children was held during the 9:30 A.M. and 11:00 A.M. worship services. The new "Jam Plan" includes a 9:00 A.M. traditional worship service, Sunday school at 10:00 A.M., and an alternate, less formal worship experience at 11:00. At the alternate service, the chancel choir does not sing. Instead, there is special music, including orchestration, and the pastors do not wear robes. The change is to involve more people in worship, music, and study. Children and youth now can attend worship, and adults will have an opportunity for study. The creativity, which has characterized the congregation in envisioning the new sanctuary and in finding ways to cover the indebtedness despite high interest rates, will not be used for outreach. Entry ports for new members often have been through a weekday Montessori school, a latchkey day-care program, a private elementary school, and a Head Start program for underprivileged children. In addition, some community programs help new residents become familiar with the church and its facilities. These include an exercise program, Theos (They Help Each Other Spiritually), and a group for widows and widowers.

Fellowship opportunities for church members include supper clubs, "L Plus" (for persons 50 and over), a 4-5-6 Club for elementary children, United Methodist Women, Retired Men, youth activities, and fellowship coffees between the two worship experiences.

In discussing their reasons for choosing Anoka Church new members mention vital worship, including excellent sermons and a fine music program, and the warmth of the congregation. These characteristics reflect the "authentic growth" philosophy of the senior pastor expressed in a brochure for current and prospective members:

> Authentic growth occurs in a congregation when three concepts are kept in sharp focus. First, the leadership must be Christ-centered; second, the congregation should be relationally styled; and third, we must deal

with people holistically. Integrated faith has to do with all of life. . . . I believe we ought to grow in depth and size, but most of all, I want us to grow in love. My friends, we are on the verge of a new day and we will be a part of a great, growing movement. I am glad to share in this exciting venture of faith with so many loving people as you.

Wendland's dreams for the church are shared by the church leaders we met. Specifically these dreams are that the church become a center for learning; be attuned to the needs of people, especially those going through crises; become the focal point of community activities; and build a residence for older adults. Other dreams are that the alternate worship experience will provide more excitement in worship for an ever-growing number of persons; that a strong senior adult program will be put into place; and that Anoka Church will become known as a center for caring.

If the members can follow their philosophy, if they can refocus from debt retirement to outreach, and if they can become more intentional in meeting needs, then the sky is the limit for this caring church, which is strategically located in the second fastest growing county in Minnesota.

GRACE UNITED METHODIST CHURCH

NAPERVILLE, ILLINOIS

Arthur Landwehr, Senior Pastor

Expecting Naperville, Illinois, to be a pleasant bedroom community for Chicago, we were stunned to learn of its explosive growth. Indeed, Naperville is often called the Silicon Valley of the Midwest. Offices for research and development for many large companies are located there.

Grace United Methodist Church, one of the five fastest growing churches in the North Central Jurisdiction, is fortunate to be located in a growing suburban area of a growing city. The church's decision to move out of downtown Naperville came after the 1968 merger of the Methodist Church and the Evangelical United Brethren Church. Suddenly in Naperville, three United Methodist churches were located within a three-block radius. None of the other churches wanted to leave the downtown location, so members at Grace decided to take the risk.

It was a fortunate decision. Church officials were able to obtain property that is now strategically located in the center of this sprawling suburb. The sanctuary and education building are contemporary in design and built of an earthtone brick, causing them to blend beautifully into the wooded surroundings. The entire thirteen-acre campus is attractively landscaped.

Already the facilities are overcrowded. Members are in the midst of a $3.5 million capital funds campaign to provide additional classroom space and activity center. Their planning will soon need to include an enlarged or new sanctuary. Even now, two of the three Sunday morning worship services are filled to capacity.

Grace Church was officially organized in 1890 as a congregation of the Evangelical Church. The roots in Naperville go back to the arrival of the DuPages, German-speaking settlers from Ohio and Pennsylvania. A look through the current pictorial directory of this vital church still reveals many German names.

Keeping alive their German and English tradition of personal piety and social responsibility, members enter their "Second Century of Grace" under the following missional statement: "The church is the people of God in Christ: a community of disciples journeying together in faith and love; committed to serve God and all people; united by our worship; proclaiming and witnessing to the Good News; growing in Christian faith, understanding, fellowship, and compassionate service. Thanks be to God."

After a successful thirteen and a half year pastorate at First Church, Evanston, Illinois, Arthur Landwehr came to Grace Church as senior pastor in July 1988. He is knowledgeable about and in touch with this energetic congregation. Lay leadership has given him high commendation, especially in preaching and administration.

He seems to have a good sense of who he is and some strong feelings about the direction he would like the church to take. He balances his intensity of feeling with a marvelous sense of humor and an easy acceptance of differing opinions.

Though the staff is small for this size congregation, the staff members are unusually competent and well trained. Their diversity of talent brings a good balance of leadership. As the church leaders plan for the future, they plan to staff for growth in order to avoid staff burnout.

Equally impressive as the staff is the well-educated and committed corps of lay leaders. This is doubly commendable since this predominantly upper middle management congregation is very mobile. One impressive ministry is the St. Andrews visitation group who, along with the minister of discipleship, has a thorough follow-up of first-time visitors and training of new members.

A strong emphasis is placed upon programming for children and youth in this family-oriented community. The minister of youth has outlined a full year of confirmation classes for eighth grade students before they are confirmed in May or early June. Though young people enjoy many retreats and fun activities, this group is especially mission oriented.

Many work regularly in the local shelter for the homeless, and last summer, 48 of their group went on a work project to Appalachia.

The annual vacation Bible school is an excellent outreach ministry. Last summer 400 children were enrolled in the unique replica of life in Bible times. Twelve tents representing the 12 tribes of Israel were set up on a vacant lot beside the church and on a major thoroughfare. The director of Christian education has plans for increasing attendance in Sunday school—especially for adults—and is enlarging the church's preschool program.

Unusually fine newspaper coverage of the church's activities, written by the director of program, gives Grace United Methodist Church high visibility in the community. Through the efforts of a part-time staff person in membership, there is a high degree of assimilation of new members and use of talents in the selection of lay leadership through the nominating committee.

If the church can be successful in increasing its facilities, broadening its financial base, and continuing its emphasis upon worship, education, and social responsibility, an increasing number of Christian disciples will move into "a new century of grace," and will stand in the gap for God in Illinois.

SOUTH CENTRAL JURISDICTION

FIRST UNITED METHODIST CHURCH

FORT WORTH, TEXAS

H. Barry Bailey, Senior Pastor

"The only churches growing in our denomination are conservative churches." If laity or clergy believe this assertion, they should visit the third fastest growing church in our denomination, the over 9,100-member First United Methodist Church in Fort Worth, Texas. The church saw a net gain in membership of 4,000 between 1976 and 1989, and its colorful pastor, H. Barry Bailey, would never be called conservative. The lay leaders characterize the membership as being theologically diverse.

What holds the long-established, diverse congregation together and enables it to grow? First, it has a history that stretches back more than 100 years into Fort Worth's own rich heritage. The first church building was a one-room church erected in 1873 for $750. Ground was broken for the present Gothic-style sanctuary on October 29, 1929, the day of the stock market crash. Some were concerned that the undertaking was too ambitious in light of the nation's economic condition. First Methodist leaders in that day (as well as today) were visionary risk takers and people of strong faith. The first worship service in the new building (the first million dollar building erected in Fort Worth) took place on June 14, 1931. Today, First Church occupies a six-block area, with buildings valued in excess of $15 million.

The leaders have continued to be bold and innovative. First Church was the first congregation to broadcast worship services—in 1922—and was one of the first Methodist churches to be broadcast live every Sunday into a multistate area. In addition, First Church was the first Methodist congregation to have a board of education, a practice which was later adopted throughout the church, and its Sunday school was the first to have graded classes that correspond with the public school system.

The church has been fortunate to have outstanding senior pastors, and the current senior pastor is no exception. A man of great warmth and personal charm, Barry Bailey is a communicator. Extremely articulate, he is a great story-teller and has a good sense of humor. He describes his preaching style as educational and issue-oriented. He takes strong stands on controversial issues and does so without polarizing the congregation. He has won the respect of the congregation and continues to relate to members in personal ways. He always introduces his opinions by saying something such as: "This is the way I feel about this issue, and I could be wrong. I encourage you to think for yourself." He never presents his opinion as the only way to look at an issue. As a result, he has won many people who had come to think that what they heard at church was simplistic or irrelevant.

Bailey's appeal to a large television audience is one of the best evangelistic tools of the church. The people who see him on television visit the church because they already feel comfortable with the service. After persons visit, they are immediately contacted by the minister of evangelism and one of 45 lay telephone callers. On the Sunday they join the church, persons meet with the minister of evangelism and the director of volunteer ministries, who try to place the new members in volunteer service in the church or community. Persons come to the church because of the preaching, but they stay because they become involved in any of a number of dynamic programs.

Throughout the years, First United Methodist Church has been recognized as a church that meets community needs. First Methodist Mission, a recently renovated building located two blocks from the church, provides a department store atmosphere for a neighborhood clothing bank. Clothing and shoes are attractively displayed, and pleasant fitting rooms are provided. The neighborhood food bank, in the same building, also approximates the atmosphere of a grocery store, as persons are served with dignity. Other community service programs provide infant formula to needy babies, after-school clubs for children and youth, and assistance to individuals and families in need. The community services that have moved to the newly renovated building have enabled space in Epworth Hall, built in the 1950s as a recreation center for youth, to be returned to its original purpose. As a result, the youth program is now building on the strength of the children's division and promises a helpful ministry to teenagers and their families in these important years of their lives.

The senior pastor has put together a superb staff of 40 persons—8 clergy, 12 program staff, and 19 support staff. The most recent addition, a director of children's ministries, has been so effective in setting up a Sunday and weekday program and in involving parental leadership that the average attendance for children in Sunday school increased from 486 to 538 in a two-year period. An unusual staff position is "minister of teaching." The man in this position received a doctorate from Yale University and taught in a seminary before joining the staff. In addition to having administrative responsibility for singles, he conducts a regular weeknight series on Bible study and theology.

A second innovative position is "director of publications." The woman in this position has a degree in journalism. She edits sermons and books for the senior pastor, does all the writing and layout of the weekly church paper, and develops brochures that go to church members. As a result, the church's publicity is professionally done.

The church has a large endowment fund, the interest from which can be used for building maintenance and renovation without affecting the operating budget.

Fort Worth's First United Methodist Church is an exciting place. Members want to enlarge their ministry and erect new educational space as the church continues to grow. A good test of the church's strength will come at the time of the senior pastor's retirement in five or six years. With faith in Christ and the continuing strong involvement of members in ministry, there is every reason to believe that this congregation will continue to be a vital witness.

HIGHLAND PARK UNITED METHODIST CHURCH

DALLAS, TEXAS

Leighton Farrell, Senior Pastor

Experiencing Highland Park United Methodist Church in Dallas, Texas, is exhilarating. One feels as if one had discovered a magnificent jewel in an unexpected place. Upon meeting the staff, experiencing the warmth of the members, and seeing the breadth and depth of ministry, one understands more of the church's greatness.

Highland Park is an old, established church, which was organized in 1916 and has met in the same sanctuary since 1926. The church has increased membership every year since 1972, growing from 7,979 that year to 12,009 in 1987. Significantly, the growth occurred while the denomination as a whole was losing members and while the Highland Park residential area was declining in population (from 10,133 in 1970 to 8,700 in 1987).

A number of factors have brought about the phenomenal growth, but much of it can be attributed to the leadership of Leighton Farrell, who has served as senior pastor since 1972. His administrative skills are a great asset for the church, and his background in research and development has enabled him to understand national trends and to blend them with church programs. One example is the establishment of a strong singles' program at Highland Park well before there was national awareness of the increasing number of single people in our culture. Similarly, Farrell developed an excellent program for couples and preschool children when he foresaw that the baby boomers would return to church with their children. He also staffed an older adult program in recognition that Americans are living much longer now than in any other century.

The senior pastor has the additional ability to choose staff members wisely and to allow them the freedom to manage their individual ministries. Though he is accessible and supportive of the staff, no one questions that Farrell is the "chief executive officer" and that each person is accountable to him as well as to God. The long tenure of staff members is evidence of the effectiveness of his management.

Farrell believes that the first requirement of a church staff should be Christian commitment and that other requirements involve character, integrity, dependability, and loyalty. "You can't learn those things, but you can acquire job skills," he says. When asked about the characteristics of a successful senior pastor of a growing church, he replied: "In addition to commitment and character, I would add hard work and caring about people. Also, the senior pastor cannot have strong ego needs if he or she is going to work well with a multiple staff."

The staff at Highland Park Church is composed of 12 ordained ministers, seven diaconal ministers, eight lay professionals, 12 support staff, 14 secretaries, six kitchen workers, 12 custodians, and 50 persons who work with the weekday child development center. Because each staff person is highly motivated, even the buildings and grounds are clean and well-kept, which is not an easy feat as over 900 meetings a month are held in the buildings.

Out of the multitude of ministries, three are especially distinctive. The assimilation program for new members is impressive. On the Sunday they join the church, new members are interviewed by members of the assimilation committee. They are asked to review volunteer opportunities and to indicate their talents and interests. The assimilation layperson puts the information on a computer and sends a memo to the appropriate staff. Staff members then contact the new members and invite them to participate where there is a need. When a new member finds a place of service, the staff member reports to the assimilation committee, which stays in touch with the new member for a year or until the member is fully assimilated. An indication of how well this program has worked is the increase in the number of volunteers—from 2,100 to over 3,000.

A second distinctive area of ministry is the child development program. In 1972, when Farrell was appointed to the church, the average age of the membership was 66. Since then, the church has been targeting young adults, and the average age of members is now 39. In 1987, of the 629 new members received, 76.3 percent were age 40 or younger; 52.3 percent were 30 or younger. Because the majority of these new members were parents (either two-parent or single-parent families) of young children, a quality child development program was essential. Today, Highland Park has child care from 7:00 A.M. to 6:00 P.M.; morning classes for children, ages two to five; and afternoon parent's day out for children, ages six months to five years. The program has a long waiting list, and 340 children are enrolled.

The older adult program is equally impressive. Out of a membership of over 12,000 persons, 2,100 are age 60 or older. In addition to Sunday school classes, the senior adult council has developed a program that includes travel (26 one-day trips and 6 overnight or weeklong trips); an elderhostel held at a camp owned by the church; and a year-round program called "Tuesday Adventures," which features such morning classes as exercise, conversational French, current events, and creative writing. After lunch, card games are available for those who wish to stay. An average of 470 persons attended "Tuesday Adventures" in 1987. An additional program is offered once a month for the frail elderly; "Care Canteen" features speakers, fellowship, and a hot meal, and transportation is provided.

The focus of Highland Park United Methodist Church has never been just on the congregation. In addition to annual support of World Service and local and foreign missions, the members have helped establish 26 other United Methodist churches, one of which—Lover's Lane—has over 7,000 members. In 1987, 80 families from Highland Park volunteered to become a part of the organizing congregation of St. Andrew's United Methodist Church in Plano, Texas. Financial resources in the amount of $100,000 a year for three years will be given for the support of the new congregation, which at the end of its second year had more than 1,000 members.

Highland Park United Methodist Church is not only a church of vision in its own right; it has also found ways to extend this vision to other congregations as well.

BEAR CREEK UNITED METHODIST CHURCH

HOUSTON, TEXAS

Robert E. Long, Senior Pastor

Defying church growth rules about location and facilities, Bear Creek United Methodist Church in Houston, Texas, is growing by leaps and bounds. It grew from a membership of 206 in 1979 to 3,318 in 1989. The average worship attendance grew from 119 to approximately 1,000. Although the location was well chosen by a conference committee, the site is off the highway. Only the cross atop the sanctuary can be seen from the state highway. A familiar rule of church growth is that the facilities need to be visible.

Another such rule is that facilities must adequately house the congregation. The theory is that if persons feel too crowded, they will go elsewhere. Until the new sanctuary was completed, Bear Creek had only two relatively small permanent buildings: an all-purpose room used for worship (with adjacent classrooms) and a children's building. Two "pre-fab" buildings were used as office space for the staff.

One thing that kept members from growing discouraged by overcrowding was the promise of their new sanctuary, which was completed in 1988. Bear Creek is a congregation of young to middle adults, most of whom have small children and a home mortgage. Yet, excited about their church, most give sacrificially of their time and resources. Despite a drastic drop in oil prices with its resultant recession in Houston's oil-dependent economy, the members at Bear Creek completed building their sanctuary. A number of church members had lost jobs or homes, yet 90 percent of the congregation participated in underwriting the operating budget and building fund.

The catalyst for all this excitement was Gerald R. (Randy) Mullikin, the senior pastor from 1979 to 1988. Lay and clergy alike responded to his conversational, personal, and practical preaching style. To grow a church, he said: "Be evangelistic, work hard, and organize for spontaneity."

Staff members of Bear Creek are competent and caring. In their relationships with one another, they model redemptive caring. Such bonding among the staff didn't just happen. They planned for it. In addition to an annual planning retreat, staff members participate in spiritual life retreats and study retreats.

The ministries that are especially strong at Bear Creek include evangelism (the care of visitors, recruitment, and the assimilation of new members), caring ministry, prayer ministry, music programs, and children's ministry.

The evangelism work area is composed of members who have joined within the past year. The theory is that the people who have most recently joined will be most enthusiastic about reaching others. First-time visitors are welcomed that same Sunday afternoon by a church member who lives in their neighborhood. The member stops by their home to deliver a visitor packet of information on church programs and Sunday school classes, a recent newsletter, a magnet with the church logo, and a complimentary dinner ticket for Wednesday night fellowship. Follow-up is made to deal with needs expressed by the visitor.

On each Monday, a list of Sunday's visitors is given to the minister of evangelism, who gives the names to 45 laypersons to make welcoming phone calls to the visitors. After a third visit to the church, a visitor receives another call and an invitation to Sunday school and other activities. Sometimes a visitor requests a visit from a pastor before joining, but most often laypersons do the visiting.

The assimilation work area is different from evangelism. When a prospect joins the church, the director of assimilation stands at the altar with him or her. Afterward, the member has a picture made for the church paper and the bulletin board. Each new member fills out a membership card, and receives a New Member Information Packet. A representative from a Sunday school class visits new members in their home within two weeks after they join to welcome them and invite them to Sunday school. The new members are invited to an orientation class and dessert fellowship within one month of the time they join. The two-hour session is led by the senior pastor during Wednesday Night Fellowship. The work area on assimilation has an elaborate system of checking the involvement of new members during their first year of membership.

The church has a strong children's ministry, with approximately 900 children enrolled in Sunday school. The church staff includes two competent women who direct the day-school program, Sunday school, and related activities. The day school has received a superior rating and has a long waiting list.

Sunday school for all ages is offered both at 9:30 and 11:00 A.M., simultaneous with worship services, as well as 8:15 A.M. classes. By emphasizing adult Sunday school during the past year, Bear Creek has increased average worship attendance by 100 and average Sunday school attendance by 200.

A new, vital program initiated in the fall of 1989 is called "Wednesday Night Fellowship." The church found a need to expand Sunday school and Bible study beyond Sunday morning due to crowded classroom facilities. The church also wanted to focus on the importance of a family's spending time together by consolidating activities to one night at the church. An average of 300 people of all ages attend classes, choirs, and fellowship on Wednesday evenings as a family growing in faith together.

The Stewardship program enables a member to fulfill his or her pledge to support the church with "prayers, presence, gifts and service." The pledge card allows for a specific commitment in each of these four areas. Volunteers are lifted up on a regular basis through the newsletter and by the pastors for the importance of their ministry. The office is staffed by volunteers, and a group of lay people are building a new Sunday school facility to be ready in the fall of 1990.

The members of Bear Creek United Methodist Church are continuing their spirit of excitement and caring since the arrival of current senior pastor, Robert E. Long, in 1988. New vistas of opportunity are now opening before them for the future.

MEMORIAL DRIVE UNITED METHODIST CHURCH

HOUSTON, TEXAS

H. Eugene Cragg, Senior Pastor

First impressions are important to persons visiting a church. If you belong to a church or even if you visit regularly, you become oblivious to things that are apparent to a first-time visitor. Churches that wish to grow should have members of their long-range planning committee try to see their church (buildings and ministries) through the eyes of a first-time visitor.

From the heavily traveled Memorial Drive in Houston, the buildings of Memorial Drive United Methodist Church are highly visible. When the church was established in 1958, the visionary founding pastor recruited 149 persons to begin meeting in a public school building. Together, they envisioned a large-membership church in the growing suburban community. They recognized the need to purchase a large lot on Memorial Drive to provide visibility. Today, the cluster of English Tudor-style buildings on nine and a half acres is valued at more than $14 million. Scattered among the buildings, which are joined by open cloisters, are huge trees from which Spanish moss hangs. It is an impressive sight for newcomers.

First-time visitors can easily find their way because the buildings are well marked. Greeters are stationed at each entrance, and information booths are located in one of the cloisters and in the administrative and educational buildings. On the front of each booth is a sign written in red calligraphy that reads, "Ask about Sunday school classes." The person in the booth tells visitors about the classes and gives them a list with descriptions of the classes and a map. Visitors feel they are wanted at Memorial Drive.

Sunday school attendance increased from 300 in 1965 to 1,091 in 1985; worship attendance increased from 694 in one service in 1965 to 1,727 in three duplicate services in 1985. The worship services have beauty and dignity, balanced by warmth and a feeling of family. The beauty is evident in the relatively new sanctuary with its stained glass windows and red carpet. The red robes worn by some of the officiating clergy and the huge floral arrangement on the altar table add even more beauty. The plaster walls combined with brick and wood provide a feeling of warmth. The element of dignity is provided by the choir processional, the familiar liturgy, and the magnificent 80-voice choir.

Music is one of the strong ministries of the church. The chancel choir is one of seven choirs and three handbell groups under the direction of the minister of music, who has served the church for 27 years. Although he uses variety in music for worship, he is not an "amplified, electronic guitar" kind of man, and the congregation seems to appreciate that. Each year, the choir presents a full-scale musical at a "dinner theater" in the church's great hall. Among the musicals presented recently have been *South Pacific*, *Oklahoma*, and *The Cotton Patch Gospel*.

The senior pastor, Eugene Cragg, has been at Memorial Drive Church for over 19 years. Loved and respected by the congregation, he is a good preacher with strong organizational skills. In the service of worship, his sermon is topical, well-organized, and practical. In sermon presentation, in the announcements, and in the reception of new members, he brings a feeling of warmth and inclusiveness to the service.

One evidence of the continued vision and adaptability of the congregation is the way members transformed a tragedy into a triumph. On Palm Sunday evening in 1980, the fellowship hall (which had been used for years as a sanctuary) and the adjacent classrooms were badly damaged by fire. Because they were in their new sanctuary by that time, they chose not to rebuild exactly what they had lost. Instead, they built a family-life center, which has space for racquetball, volleyball, basketball, an exercise and game room, classrooms, a great hall, kitchen facilities, and a chapel. This congregation is not guilty of doing things as they have always done them.

Even now, a long-range planning committee is doing demographic studies of the community and looking at the projected growth of Houston. In addition, the committee is evaluating the church and targeting needed areas of growth for the next decade. One of its surprising discoveries is that, although the community is not growing and its residents are getting older, the average age of the church membership is getting younger due to an influx of young couples with children and an increasing number of single adults.

One of the best entry points for young families is an excellent children's program on Sundays and weekdays. The congregation takes great care in recruiting and training teachers for Sunday school and vacation Bible school. The average children's attendance in Sunday school in 1987 was 450 (225 preschool and 225 elementary). About 350 children were enrolled in vacation Bible school; 580 in summer day camps (for kindergarten through fifth grade); and 451 in "Five Summer Days" (for ages six months to five years). There is always a waiting list for the day-school program. Three hundred children are enrolled either in the preschool or mother's day out programs. Another 75 children come from nearby schools for "creative care," an extended day care.

Family life and youth ministries are under the same umbrella, and a team of five professionals leads this program involving hundreds of individuals. A full range of athletics is provided, including 12 basketball teams, 14 baseball teams, 11 soccer teams, and a number of tournaments for handball, Ping-Pong, and bowling. The youth ministry focuses on study and outreach as well as recreation. The highlight of the senior high program would be the annual work camp, involving 80 high-schoolers. Recent trips to Appalachia, Louisiana, and San Antonio have provided meaningful experiences. The junior high group stays in Houston and works at Larkin Center, the inner city mission owned and operated by Memorial Drive Church.

Outreach was written into the organizing purpose of the church, and members continue to have it as one of their important goals. As a result, the church took over a district-owned community center. It totally supports and runs the center through a paid director, a staff of seven adults, and volunteers from the church. The annual budget is more than $200,000. Church members are also concerned about foreign missions. On the Sunday we attended, a young doctor from Africa, whom the church had sent through medical school, was back to say "thank you" and to ask for the continued support of his hospital in Nigeria.

A unique feature of the quality adult education program at Memorial Drive is the "Disciple Bible Study," written by the director of adult ministries. The study, which has been in existence for over eight years, draws more than 200 participants on Wednesday mornings and evenings each week. Bible study leaders are carefully chosen and trained. At the beginning of each semester, a professor of biblical studies from Southern Methodist University comes to the church for a weekend overview of the book of the Bible that study leaders will use. Each Monday morning, the leaders receive training from the director who wrote the materials and the pastor who gives the weekly lectures. The training session is interesting and true to Wesleyan theology.

The purpose of Memorial Drive United Methodist Church, as stated in the long-range planning document, is "to proclaim the good news of Christ's redeeming love so that all people may know themselves as children of God and respond to that love through decision, commitment, and mission." The church is fulfilling its purpose in a beautiful way. As it continues to live out its purpose, the church will grow even beyond its present membership of 8,200 and serve as a vital witness for Jesus Christ in a great southwestern city.

CUSTER ROAD UNITED METHODIST CHURCH

PLANO, TEXAS

W. Mark Craig, Senior Pastor

Custer Road United Methodist Church grew in membership from 350 in 1981 to 2,850 in 1990; from a worship attendance of 370 to 1,673; from a Sunday school attendance of 312 to 1,300; and from an operational budget of $215,000 to $850,000, with an additional annual average capital funds budget of $700,000. Why? How can a mainline denominational church grow so quickly when most mainline churches are declining?

First, it is a new church. The North Texas Conference recognized the need for another United Methodist congregation in a suburban area that has exploded with population growth. In 1970, the population of Plano was 17,872; in 1980, it had reached 72,331; in 1988, it reached 119,000; and Plano is still growing. The conference bought a five-acre tract of land on Custer Road, and W. Mark Craig was appointed as organizing pastor.

Much of the church's phenomenal growth is attributable to Craig's commitment, hard work, enthusiasm, and administrative and relational skills. Working out of a small, rented office, Craig contacted new residents in Plano and sent out a bulk mailing to invite people to the first worship service, which was held in the auditorium of an elementary school. Two hundred persons attended on the cold, icy February Sunday; eight of those present joined the church that day. By the end of the conference year in June, 380 persons had joined.

From the beginning, Craig delegated authority and had a high level of volunteerism, which exists to this day. Few churches of this size can carry on such a comprehensive ministry with such a limited professional staff. There are 2 ordained ministers, a full-time minister of music, a full-time youth director, a full-time business manager, and 10 part-time staff members who came from the membership of the church.

Volunteers are used in every area of ministry, but the most visible are the office volunteers who are recruited, trained, and directed by Sandy Ragland. The smoothly run office is certainly a tribute to Ragland, who is highly motivated, well-organized, sensitive, and diplomatic. All the typing (no staff person has a secretary), telephone answering, newspaper and bulletin preparation, and copying is done by volunteers.

Four goals guide the congregation: to reach the unchurched, to minister to family units, to have a strong educational program (with emphasis upon adult education), and to be a serving church.

A part of the unity of the congregation comes from a genuine understanding of and commitment to goals, as well as from an intentional decision to be a growing church. When we asked laity about their vision for the church in the next five years, they replied: "We expect to have around 5,000 members, to increase our facilities, to grow spiritually, and to expand our ministries."

The pivotal points of congregational life are the two Sunday morning worship services at 9:00 and 11:00, which the senior pastor describes as "formal, lively, but traditional with dignity." The service, which lasts 50 minutes, centers around a 15-minute sermon that is, according to the laity, "biblically based and life-oriented." Craig is a topical, not lectionary preacher. Because many members have been unchurched or have come from non-Wesleyan backgrounds, there is no use of ritual, except for the weekly inclusion of the Apostles' Creed, the Lord's Prayer, and the Gloria Patri. Great variety is displayed in the use of choral and instrumental groups, but hymns are the well-known ones.

A graduate of Perkins Theological Seminary, Donna Whitehead provides a perfect balance to Craig's preaching and pastoral skills. Whitehead is considered by the laity to be a good preacher, but she preaches only when Craig is away or when invited by neighboring United Methodist churches. Her strong administrative and organizational gifts suit this team ministry. She is responsible for adult education and all small group activities with adults.

Because of the strong emphasis on adult education, Custer Road has only one Sunday school hour to avoid competition with worship. The average age of the membership is 40; thus, only one of the 25 adult classes is for persons over 50 years of age. One woman in this group said: "We had to organize to have some identity in this young church. We have called ourselves the 'Hilltoppers.'" Two classes are for singles; the others are for young and middle adult couples. Most of the classes use the "International Lesson Series," and a strong emphasis is placed on fellowship. Social issues are the focus in the "Forum" or the "I Hate Sunday School" class.

Serious Bible study for adults takes place on Wednesday evening: more than 400 persons are enrolled in "Bethel Bible," "Serendipity," or "Kerygma" studies. Others are enrolled in the "Stephen Ministries" study or support groups. These studies are excellent vehicles for individual Bible study, training for teachers and leaders, and the assimilation of new members.

Custer Road has a good program for children, which places special attention on the cleanliness and quality of child care in the nursery. In addition, there is a lively recreation and special activities program. In the music program, the choir membership tripled after the first full-time minister of music, Tim Morrison, joined the staff. In addition to the chancel choir, he has organized four children's choirs, one youth choir, and five handbell choirs; he uses many instrumentalists in worship. People are excited about participating in this ministry of music.

The youth ministry is under the direction of a young adult who worked with youth for ten years before coming to Custer Road in June 1989. John Baldwin is able to have fun with the youth on their level, or he can speak to them from an adult perspective.

In addition to an excellent education program for the youth, their Sunday evening program involves over 100 junior- and senior-high youth in such activities as choir, snack suppers, studies by individual classes, and group recreation. The program is unique in that it is based on service, not recreation. The council is not made up of president and vice-president, but of servant-leader teams that include each youth. The youth plan, promote, and participate regularly in local mission projects. Twice a year, they are involved in out-of-state service projects.

The young people say, "We have fun, but mostly through service to others." The confirmation class is done through the youth division because it is for seventh instead of sixth graders.

The church has had tremendous growth in its 10-year history. As it becomes a superchurch of 5,000 to 10,000 members, its leaders will consider having duplicate Sunday schools, as well as worship services, and have some form of weekday preschool or child care.

ST. LUKE'S UNITED METHODIST CHURCH

HOUSTON, TEXAS

James W. Moore, Senior Pastor

The beautiful Georgian buildings of St. Luke's United Methodist Church are located on 15 landscaped acres in a prestigious section of Houston. Just down the street from the church is the Galleria, one of the world's largest covered shopping malls. A few blocks in the opposite direction is River Oak Boulevard, which has some magnificent homes. There, in the midst of great affluence, is the church being the church. As with the Christ it represents, St. Luke's is attracting people of all ages and needs.

In 1945, several families who lived in River Oaks attended First United Methodist Church in downtown Houston, but they decided they needed a United Methodist congregation in their neighborhood. With the endorsement of the Houston Southwest District and the Texas Conference, the families purchased the land where the church now stands. Durwood Fleming was appointed as the founding pastor, and on November 11, 1945, the church was organized with 220 charter members. Today, the membership exceeds 8,500; Sunday school enrollment is over 3,300.

From the beginning, the founders decided against limiting the church's outreach by organizing just a suburban church. They named it St. Luke's instead of the "River Oaks Church" to emphasize its metropolitan, even regional, outreach. Now, 45 years later, the church has many fourth generation families who drive long distances to attend the church.

The visionaries who founded the church were determined that St. Luke's would not be a "silk-stocking" church, but a serving church. Church members today carry out the founder's vision. In 1987, church members gave $1 million to serve others, which is $1.00 for every $3.00 they spent on property and programs. In 1990, they plan to contribute $1.00 toward service of others for every $2.00; by the year 2000, members hope to give $1.00 to others for every $1.00 they spend on themselves.

One of the church's service projects is the Houston Project. In 1987, church members gave $175,000 to this project, which provides funds for such causes as the Salvation Army, the Lighthouse for the Blind, a homeless shelter, and a smaller church that needed help raising funds for an educational building. Requests for funds come to a standing committee, whose members award funds in increments of $10,000 or more. A similar project, called the Outreach Council, annually provides $75,000 in increments of up to $10,000 for emergency needs.

James (Jim) Moore is the youngest senior pastor the church has had. He followed Walter Underwood, who was elected to the episcopacy in 1984. Moore won the affection of the congregation through his sincerity, his ability to relate to all types of people, and his preaching style, which is conversational and life-oriented. He is not a lectionary preacher, although he does preach the church year. His book, *Seizing the Moments* (published by Abingdon Press), is a written example of his interesting preaching style. The book was chosen by *Guideposts* as one of the 1988 book selections.

The philosophy of the church, as summarized by Moore, has three parts. First, there ought to be a church somewhere that is doing it right. . . . St. Luke's wants to be that church. Second, St. Luke's wants always to be the Body of Christ—teaching, preaching, healing, caring, and loving. Third, members of St. Luke's want to be intentional in all their ministries. Some churches saunter into programming with the attitude, "If we are a good church, people will join." People at St. Luke's believe that they have to be intentional in inviting and reaching others, in serving others, and in having inspirational worship and effective ministries.

The competent members of St. Luke's staff (clergy, lay professionals, and support staff) have a strong esprit de corps that is evident when persons talk with them or observe them at work. Although the church has a high level of volunteerism, the members have great respect for the staff and look to them for expertise and guidance.

The balanced ministries of St. Luke's involve all age groups. Many persons come to St. Luke's for the first time because of the varied programs, which include a television ministry, a day school for children, a youth recreation program, singles' ministries, a counseling ministry, a "Mainstreamers" program for persons 55 years or older, and "An Evening at St. Luke's." The church also has one of the finest music ministries in America, which is led by Bob Bennett. The music minister has been at the church for over 30 years and recently served on the denomination's Hymnal Revision Committee as the chairperson of the "themes" subcommittee.

Through the years, the ministry to children of St. Luke's has been of the highest quality. The large children's building seems to be exploding with preschool and elementary school children. The summer program is successful despite the humid Houston weather and family vacations. "Summer Days" for children, ages two to four, is offered three days each week of the summer. Day camp is held five days a week for children in kindergarten through the eighth grade. Vacation Bible school is also popular; 400 children and 100 workers participate. The summer programs offer learning, crafts, and recreation, and the children take full advantage of the activities building, which houses a swimming pool, a regulation-size gym, and game rooms.

Throughout the school year, St. Luke's has the largest day school for children (ages three through kindergarten) in the Texas Conference. Children up to three years of age participate in a mother's day out program. An extended-care program is offered for the children of working parents. Only 50 percent of the parents whose children attend the day school are members of St. Luke's. Only 10 percent of the extended-care participants are church members.

An increasing number of singles drive from all over the Houston area to participate in the strong fellowship for singles. Kent Kilbourne, a compassionate Christian and talented musician, leads this group. He is known at the church as the "John Denver of United Methodism."

The older adult program at St. Luke's is directed by Dean

Robinson, who developed a senior adult council and organized the 1,900 older adults at the church into a ministry called the Mainstreamers. A ministry by, for, and to older adults, the Mainstreamers program includes travel (day trips, overnight trips, and three-week trips), service (meals on wheels, transportation for the frail elderly, and a food pantry), and fellowship. Once a month, senior adults come to the church for classes, games, and lunch. A number of persons have joined the church because of the Mainstreamers program.

St. Luke's has an innovative outreach program for visitors called "An Evening at St. Luke's." Adults who visited the church during the last three months are invited to attend this quarterly dinner event. Young people greet the visitors in the parking lot and direct them to the dining room, which is decorated with candles and flowers. After receiving nametags and hors d'oeuvres, the visitors are seated at a table where a church member serves as host. After dinner, they are welcomed by the senior pastor, view a ten-minute videotape, and tour the facilities. They return to the dining room for coffee and hot cider and to visit booths for various ministries, each staffed by the appropriate person. Many persons indicate their desire to join the church that evening. Always, 75 percent of those attending the event join within the next few months.

St. Luke's is already a great church. As it continues to strengthen its ministries, accelerates its outreach, and brings a Cokesbury bookstore to the campus, it can become an even greater regional center for United Methodism.

ST. JAMES UNITED METHODIST CHURCH

LITTLE ROCK, ARKANSAS

John P. Miles, Senior Pastor

Even during a weekend when Little Rock, Arkansas, was caught in the icy grip of the worst snowstorm in 60 years, St. James United Methodist Church had its usual four worship services (one on Saturday evening). In the 10:45 A.M. Sunday service we attended, the 1,000-seat sanctuary was comfortably filled; 40 members of the choir were present.

One can easily catch the spirit of St. James because everybody (not just professional greeters) greets a visitor warmly. Therefore as visitors, we were glad we had made the effort to attend. Members of the staff—especially the senior pastor—were smiling, greeting, introducing, directing, or hugging at every turn of the corridor.

In the adult Sunday school class we attended, the president and class members conversed without the usual in-house jokes that make a visitor feel like an outsider. We heard about who was serving at the Stone Soup Kitchen and what had been done to help two families without heat. It was evident that St. James is a serving church, sensitive and responsive to human need.

The worship service was informal. The liturgist, a woman in her early forties, was an associate pastor of the church. The hymns were traditional and well chosen. Since it was Epiphany, we heard hymns such as "As with Gladness Men of Old" sung lustily and with a full organ accompaniment. During one of the hymns, we sang the first stanza, turned and greeted the people around us while the organist played the next two stanzas, then joined together in singing the last stanza.

John Miles, or "Brother John" as he is affectionately called by the congregation, preached his usual 18-minute sermon. He talked about failure and contrasted society's view of failure with the biblical view. His illustrations included some of his own failures. There was no sense of separation between the pastor and the congregation. The message was clear: We are all sinners who are forgiven and redeemed by Christ and sent forth to do Christ's work in God's world. After the benediction, the choir's vocal "sending forth" was triumphant and challenging.

We left the service confident that we would like to return. Obviously, many other visitors have had the same feeling because the church has had a net increase of 2,644 members during Miles' pastorate. The membership has grown from 695 to 3,339 in 1987.

As we talked with staff members, 15 congregational leaders, the district superintendent, and Bishop Richard B. Wilke, we concluded that the following factors have contributed to the church's success.

First, the church is located in the fastest growing area of the city. The area was carefully chosen by a district committee, and the entire project was financially supported by the conference, the district, and the Board of Global Ministries. The small group of charter members included business entrepreneurs who were accustomed to thinking big and taking risks in business; they did the same for their church. In fact, they quickly sold the 3½ acre plot chosen by the district committee and bought a 10 acre plot on which the present complex of buildings stands. In addition, they employed an architect to sketch a long-range plan, which included nine buildings. (All but three have been completed.) They intended from the beginning to be a large church.

Second, although they had an excellent founding pastor, the church didn't "take off" in membership and programs until the present pastor was appointed. Miles loves people, relating as easily to children and youth as to adults, to the poverty-stricken as well as to the "blue chippers," and to the moral outcast as well as to the morally upright. He is nonjudgmental, believing that God hasn't finished with any of us yet. That, combined with informal, vital worship and his insistence that St. James be a servant church has attracted young adults, the "baby boomers" lost to so many mainline denominations.

St. James could easily have become an affluent, suburban

church, but the pastor's dream of having all kinds of people in the church and his ability to sell that dream have helped it become a metropolitan regional church. Miles' informality (he never wears a tie unless he is "marrying, burying, or preaching"), his high energy level, his commitment to Christ and to church growth, and his desire "to keep his finger in all of the pies" have been unifying factors in congregational growth.

Third, the organizing congregation established a statement of purpose, which is referred to often in administrative board meetings and is reviewed by each long-range planning committee as it launches a new five-year program. Furthermore, each new member is given a copy of the purpose statement. The purpose, understood and agreed to by members of the congregation, includes the following goals: to continue to reach persons for Christ and church membership; to provide the appropriate staff to support the growing membership; to continue to be a servant church by reaching out to those in need; and to aid each person in the church to establish a personal relationship with God through faith in Jesus Christ.

Fourth, the church's ministries are diverse enough to attract people of varying ages and interests. Through the years, the leadership has included competent laity and professional staff. The church's most recognized program is the music ministry. The minister of music and his wife, the organist, have been with the church from the beginning. Five hundred people are involved in this ministry in eight choirs and eleven handbell groups.

Another significant program is social outreach, which includes the Stone Soup Kitchen for street people and weekly responses to needs that come through Little Rock's social service agencies. Church members are working to establish another United Methodist church in an adjacent subdivision, and they are becoming more intentional about world missions.

A number of innovative programs will likely have long-term benefits. The early Christian development for children six months to two years is used on Sunday and in the weekday school. The "Parents in Action" program provides a support group for junior and senior high United Methodist Youth Fellowship groups. (Incidentally, the staff person in this area is not called minister to youth, but minister to families with youth.) A new assimilation program will encourage even more lay involvement.

St. James United Methodist Church, which is described by Miles as an alternate to both the Jerry Falwell type church and the social gospel type church, should grow to be a "super" church. The factors enabling such growth include continuing to have a senior pastor who has preaching, relational, and administrative skills; continuing to have unity in diversity; continuing to have people-centered programs for all ages; and continuing to increase staff and lay involvement as the membership grows.

WESTERN JURISDICTION

LOS ALTOS UNITED METHODIST CHURCH

LOS ALTOS, CALIFORNIA

John L. Dodson, Senior Pastor

The senior pastor of Los Altos United Methodist Church is not afraid of taking a risk with his congregation. An exciting example happened one Sunday in 1984 when John L. Dodson decided to invite worshipers to share in a familiar parable. Dodson had received an unexpected gift of $1,000. Usually he gave such gifts to the church treasurer for special needs not covered in the church budget. But, this time, he was thinking of a single father in the congregation who had adopted twelve physically disabled children. This father needed financial help as well as pastoral support. Dodson was preparing to preach on the parable of the talents, and he saw a unique opportunity to use the gift of money. Why not break the thousand dollars into five-dollar bills, give them out to persons present at the service, and challenge the people to put their money to work as Jesus instructed the servants to do in the parable? Whatever money was returned would be placed in a fund for the family in need. Dodson's congregation was ready for the challenge. They were excited as they planned a flurry of projects and creative events.

Six weeks later $1,000 had been parlayed into $11,000. When the members turned in their money, John asked them to tell the stories of how they had earned it. Some had made ceramic and needlepoint items and sold them at craft fairs; some had made cakes, cookies, and pies and had bake sales. Two ten-year-old girls had spent a part of their money to have flyers printed, advertising their availability to do yard work and babysitting; they were glad to return their earnings of $50.00. Even visitors from as far away as Hawaii and Boston, who had attended the first service, returned the enhanced value of their five-dollar bills. Intangible results included a spirit of unity and energized excitement within the congregation and a deepened desire to reach out to others.

This innovate idea is typical of the ministry at Los Altos Church. When Dodson was appointed to the church 12 years ago, the average worship attendance was 297, and the membership was 1,100. Today this church is the fastest growing church in the Western Jurisdiction with over 2,300 members, and average attendance at the three morning worship services is 950.

All the members—charter, new, young, or old—say that Dodson has made a big difference. With a background in psychology and theology, Dodson was campus minister at the University of Nevada, Reno, while he taught bio-ethics at the University School of Medical Science. He was appointed in 1978 to Los Altos United Methodist Church. There is no doubt that he is the right man for this place and time. He loves God and people, and he seems perfectly comfortable with who he is. As perceived by the congregation, he is authentic, knowledgeable, gregarious, accepting, hard-working, and visionary. In addition, he is able to motivate the membership and mobilize them for action. Seldom does one find a congregation so unified in the love of the pastor and in vision for the church.

Additional keys to the rapid growth of this congregation include an excellent esprit de corps among staff members, each supporting the others. The staff consists of 30 persons, full and part-time. Many members of the staff were once members of the congregation who went back for further education, then joined the ministry team. Nancy Roslund, director of volunteers, directs activities for more than 1,000 volunteers in a variety of services in and beyond the church. The level of lay leadership is high and reflects the church's goal of "every member a minister." Marie Cieslak, parish visitor, has just received her M.A. from Fuller Seminary at age 73. She is active in a nursing home ministry. Roy Damonte is an experienced and skilled educator who directs a fine Christian education program for children and youth with the summer vacation Bible school. For adults the School of Christian Living is offered on Wednesday evenings. It is a program based on a similar concept at the Church of the Savior in Washington, D.C. It provides for three semesters (10 weeks) a year for basic Christian training.

An excellent music program includes six graded choirs, beginning with kindergarten-age children, two bell choirs, and a 40-piece orchestra. The Starfire Singers for senior high youth is especially popular because of its annual tours (the group will tour Russia in 1990) and original musicals. They sing every Sunday at the 9:30 or 11:15 service. One of the two adult choirs, Morning Glory, sings at the 8:00 A.M. service. The chancel choir offers great variety in the 9:30 A.M. or 11:15 A.M. worship services. All choirs perform serious musical works, such as Handel's "Messiah," as well as Broadway musicals and contemporary music.

The spiritual vitality of the congregation is evidenced by the strong emphasis upon prayer. In each Sunday worship service, worshipers are invited to write their prayer concerns and put them in the offering. This has grown from an average of eight requests in 1984 to over 100 each Sunday at present. These confidential requests are prayed for by three strong and effective prayer groups who write letters to those who share their concerns. Spiritual formation is further enhanced through Bible studies on Thursday mornings and evenings, spiritual life retreats, and many small groups.

A unique feature of the Los Altos congregation is the number of professional therapists who are members. They lead personal growth seminars and retreats throughout the year and help the senior pastor and the associate pastor, Janna Jackson, with pastoral counseling. They were of special help two years ago in assisting the congregation through its grief in the sudden death of the greatly beloved church organist, who died in a fall from a ladder while tuning the organ. They helped again by providing psychological counseling following the 1989 Loma Prieta Earthquake.

The congregation's mission outreach includes an array of local missions and the building of a church in Bolivia. When the Loma Prieta Earthquake struck on October 17, 1989, Los Altos United Methodist Church responded with a $52,000 collection and immediately sent teams to Watsonville, Boulder Creek, and Santa Cruz to assist with aid and support. The church is committed to continue work in the affected areas over the years ahead. Los Altos United Methodist Church initiated a homeless project in December 1989, opening its facilities to feed and house people in a conjoint program with other churches. Now in its sixth month, the program has been warmly embraced by the community and the churches, and over 52 percent of the people in the program have graduated to permanent jobs and housing.

Though the overall program of the church is balanced and inclusive, no one seems to feel that the congregation has "arrived." The long-range planning committee lists such goals as an enlarged Sunday school, a stronger base of financial support, greater mission outreach, better assimilation of new members, a larger staff, and continuing the strong volunteer tradition. With the addition of another associate pastor, Tom Rannells, last year, two of these goals are becoming reality. Rannells is primarily responsible for new members and their assimilation into the church programs and for the singles' group, a highly motivated group of all ages engaging in a wide variety of activities from downhill skiing to sponsoring workshops by nationally known authors. A committee is also carefully planning a lay shepherding and visitation program, which will enhance the pastoral care program. They understand themselves as "the church that reaches out," and they believe that "with God, all things are possible."

ST. ANDREW UNITED METHODIST CHURCH

LITTLETON, COLORADO

Wesley Kendall, Senior Pastor

St. Andrew United Methodist Church in Littleton, Colorado, breaks all the church growth rules about location—and continues to grow. Though the attractive stone and cedar buildings are located on a state highway in a growing area of southeast Denver, the church is somewhat hidden from view; it is possible to drive past the church several times without ever seeing it.

In addition, a large recreation center has been built on adjacent land, and the church and center share the same driveway entrance. The name of the church is listed below that of the center on a large colorful sign at the entrance. Unless you know to look for the church sign, however, you see only "Goodson Recreation Center," which is printed in bold letters.

With such poor visibility, how does this church continue to grow? Variety and excellence of program, creative worship, and personal initiative are the obvious reasons. From its beginning in 1960, the church has consistently turned its liabilities into assets. Many new congregations are established through the efforts and material resources of a larger congregation or a district or an annual conference. St. Andrew began after Mrs. Rachael Stander Low, a field worker for the Denver Methodist Church Extension Society, spent months going door to door in the newly developing southeast area to determine if there were enough Methodists to begin a new church. There were 40 persons interested enough to attend an organizational meeting September 25, 1960, in the Peabody Elementary School. The church was chartered November 17, 1960, with 60 members.

From the beginning there has been strong lay involvement and a sense of ownership for church policy and program. Though there has been, and currently is, excellent clergy and staff leadership, policies of the church have been made by competent laity. Perhaps one of the reasons for the church's success has been the continuing commitment on the part of staff and laity to do more for others than for themselves. They were commissioned to do this by Mrs. Low, who suggested the name of St. Andrew for the disciple who brought his brother to Jesus. She believed that the congregation would bring people to Christ and do more for others than for themselves.

One of the outstanding examples of this selflessness is the way in which the congregation put both human and material resources into the organization of St. Luke United Methodist Church in an adjacent neighborhood. In fact, in 1983, members at St. Andrew voted to postpone their own badly needed building expansion and give $250,000 to their sister church. As Jesus promised, "Give and it shall be given unto you." St. Andrew has been blessed not only with enlarged membership but with expanded buildings as well.

The growth in membership came largely after the arrival of Russ Brown as senior pastor in 1974. He was personable, enthusiastic, an outstanding preacher, and an excellent recruiter with an ability to empower laity for ministry. Under his leadership church officials made a decision to be intentional about reaching others for Christ and church membership. During his 12-year pastorate, the Christian education program increased, with special emphasis upon adult education; the mission outreach was enlarged and personalized, with adult teams being sent to Mexico City and youth teams to Mission Service in the United States; the staff was greatly enlarged; special emphasis was given to creative worship; and variety of music was presented by five choirs and other musical groups.

After Brown left in 1987, the church was extremely fortunate to have Wesley Kendall appointed as senior pastor. While serving as the Rocky Mountain Conference Council Director, he had attended St. Andrew, so he knew most of the members and is a close friend of Brown. As a result, he not only has brought energy and enthusiasm to the church's continuing ministries, but has added new ones as well.

Spiritual depth of staff and laity and a spirit of caring are obvious even during a brief visit. Great warmth is evident as members greet each other and newcomers in the large narthex before and after worship. In addition, the church is organized for caring, with each member being part of a neighborhood care unit; also a large number of persons are trained for the Stephen's Ministry.

Perhaps more than any other one experience, the creative worship experience symbolizes the essence of this dynamic congregation. On the Sunday we visited we found the following: the music was lively and varied; the inclusiveness of the congregation was seen as a female pastor led the service and was assisted by two laypersons; a short film on inclusiveness was followed by the children's story on "The Good Shepherd"; and a time was provided for congregational sharing of joys and concerns. All of this was pulled together in a short, succinct, and effective sermon by the senior pastor, calling the congregation to be the people of God.

We left the worship experience feeling what many visitors must feel. The church may be landlocked and difficult to find, but it's surely worth the effort. It's no surprise that the church continues to grow.

TRINITY UNITED METHODIST CHURCH

DENVER, COLORADO

James Barnes, Senior Pastor

"He was the right man at the right place at the right time." Though that may have been said about many persons through the years, it certainly is true of the 1980 appointment of James E. Barnes as senior pastor of Trinity United Methodist Church in Denver, Colorado.

Barnes is the right man because he is a transformational leader. In addition to being an excellent preacher, he has administrative and relational skills that allow members to share his vision, no matter how unorthodox or revolutionary. His optimism, courage to make hard decisions, and high energy level, combined with his professional skills, inspire a congregation to follow joyously.

The place was right because the church was ready for his kind of leadership. In the decade and a half before his arrival, morale had zoomed to an all-time low as the membership, the finances, the program, and the spirit had deteriorated. But a corps of dedicated leaders and committed members simply wouldn't let the church die. So, Trinity was the right place for Barnes' leadership.

The time was right because, despite the low morale in the church, an economic boom was taking place in downtown Denver where the church is located. Even before Barnes' arrival, the church had been contacted by several real estate developers about selling the church property. The church was offered handsome prices, but each offer involved selling the church building; loyal members had no intention of selling or of relocating.

In the fall, about six months after he arrived at Trinity, Barnes was walking back to the church from a luncheon. That day, as on most other days, he was thinking about the future of Trinity. As he gazed at the historic structure, he saw, with a sudden burst of insight, that the biggest asset the church possessed was airspace. Perhaps the Trinity educational building (rebuilt after a disastrous fire in 1966), which was adjacent to the sanctuary, might be sold for airspace. The members didn't have the same emotional attachment to it that they had for the historic sanctuary. Money received from its sale could restore the sanctuary and provide education space below ground. He and members of the board of trustees began to put out feelers to their business contacts.

In the beautifully written and illustrated history of the church, *Heritage of Heroes*, Linda Kirby, wrote: "In early 1981, J. Richard Shiff, C.E.O. of Bramalea, a development company headquartered in Toronto, Canada, approached Trinity. Both Shiff and Bramalea are known as being progressive and socially responsible and Shiff is also a dedicated religious man. The company had developed housing areas in Canada which included open space for schools long before zoning boards thought of requiring such agreements."

Shiff and Bramalea had also managed at least one development that included the restoration and preservation of a church in the midst of the property. They were vitally interested in getting into the downtown Denver real estate market. They convinced the church leadership that their company had what was necessary to reach an agreement with the church. Trinity's airspace would enable them to nearly double the height of their proposed office building.

The outcome is breathtakingly beautiful. The church's Plaza Center consists of two floors underground with a large atrium opening from the street all the way down to the second underground floor. The building includes staff offices, classrooms, chapel, parlors, and a bride's room. The building opens into a piaza with flower beds. Above, it is covered with a beautiful green grass area. Both are used for fellowship and recreational activities.

In addition to constructing this building, Bramalea paid for demolishing the old education building, completely renovating the sanctuary, which included new heating and airconditioning systems. The space below the sanctuary, which is at street level, was renovated to include a large, restaurant-equipped kitchen, a small dining room, a large fellowship hall, two new restrooms, practice and robing rooms for the choirs, and a large elevator to stop at all five levels of the building and the sanctuary building. Trinity received a guarantee of 500 parking spaces on Sunday and 100 on weeknights, with 12 allotted for staff, in the adjoining parking garage. Last, but not least, was a $2 million endowment fund.

Obviously, facilities do not make a church. But from the day of his arrival, Barnes began to look for new people to join Trinity Church. He also began to staff for growth. Today the church is alive and vibrant. The membership has gone from 1,106 in 1980, when Barnes was appointed, to 2,150 in 1989. Members are involved and working in community outreach and missions. In addition, the church building is used seven days a week by communiy groups such as Alcoholics Anonymous, aerobics, Junior League, Denver Chamber Orchestra, and A.A.U.W. Between 100 and 150 weddings are held in the sanctuary each year. Most of these are performed by the senior pastor. Because of the warmth and hospitality they experience from staff members and the beauty of the sanctuary, many of the couples decide to make Trinity their church home.

"Accent on excellence" might be aptly applied to the various ministries and programs at the church. Lay leaders and staff are keenly aware that 98 percent of their members drive past as many as eight to twelve other Methodist churches in order to attend Trinity. The church's uniqueness, by design, is to insist on excellence in preaching, in printing (their bulletins and brochures are first-class), and in programming.

The music ministry, the singles' ministry, and adult education are especially outstanding. There is a good children's ministry, but the church expects both it and the youth ministry to expand with the imminent arrival of a new staff person in Christian education.

No church can have stable growth without a thorough plan of recruitment. At Trinity, a visitor would find it difficult to attend worship or Sunday school on any given Sunday and not receive a telephone call from a layperson by Sunday evening.

First, the visitor registers on the ritual of friendship pad in worship. If visitors do not sign the registry, they are usually spotted and met by one of the assigned "pew greeters." Names of Sunday school visitors and names that appear on offering envelopes are telephoned to the minister of evangelism. By 5:30 P.M. a group of lay members of the evangelism work area arrive at the church to telephone that day's visitors.

On Monday, a letter, containing a handsome bookmark with an embossed image of the church and signed by both the senior pastor and the minister of evangelism, is mailed to each of the first-time visitors. By Thursday, and no later than Friday, they receive a call from the minister of evangelism.

A four-week membership class for new members and those who are considering membership is held regularly during the Sunday school hour. On the fourth Sunday, there is a breakfast at the church and an orientation session, which includes a professionally produced video depicting the life and the ministries of the church. At this session a "Trinity Friend" is assigned to each new family or single. These friends keep in contact with the new members for three months or until they have become assimilated into the life of the church. New members also attend a dessert party hosted by Jim and Mary Barnes held on a Sunday evening.

A relatively new staff person, a coordinator of volunteers, is making it possible for all members to volunteer for service for the amount of time they have to give. Trinity staff members believe that serving members are active members.

No write-up of this great church could be complete without a salute to Jean Kirby, the secretary to the senior pastor and church administrator. For 28 years, she has been the glue that has held the organization together. She is a deeply committed Christian whose job skills and loyalty to the senior pastor are equalled by her love of the people. She is sensitive to their needs and problems and is always on hand to greet, comfort, answer questions, and hug.

In reading the compelling history of Trinity Church and seeing its present dynamism, it seems obvious that God's hand is on this great church. In the words of the visionary senior pastor, "And the end is not yet in sight."

FIRST UNITED METHODIST CHURCH

PHOENIX, ARIZONA

DeWane Zimmerman, Senior Pastor

In an admittedly secular society, why would anyone go to church, especially in Phoenix, Arizona, where there are sunny skies 300 days a year and where the average temperature is 87.6° high and 63.7° low? If you were a member of or a visitor to First United Methodist Church there, you would go to church because of the church climate of warmth, caring, and acceptance, and because worship is a beautiful celebration of the God who was revealed in Jesus Christ.

The focal point for these weekly worship celebrations is the sermon presented by a highly relational and much beloved senior pastor, DeWane Zimmerman. Church leaders, staff members, new church members, and members of differing age groups list "DeWane's preaching" as the number one strength of the church. Biblically based but oriented to the everyday life situations of the members, the sermons are communicated on a feeling as well as a thinking level. Zimmerman speaks in a conversational tone, uses humor appropriately, and uses no notes. Each listener has the feeling that he is speaking directly to her or him.

Zimmerman (or D.Z. as he is affectionately called), has a powerful pulpit presence. The worshiper feels that this man knows who he is and whose he is, and is happy about both. In addition, he is well read and draws illustrations easily from classical literature, contemporary events, as well as from the Bible. In fact, his biblical knowledge, blending with an almost uncanny understanding of the human condition, makes the message seem as current as the morning newspaper.

The entire worship experience flows beautifully and easily. From the prelude through the benediction, there are no awkward pauses. The music, prayers, scripture, greeting, and sermon blend harmoniously into a moving assurance of God's presence and grace.

Yet, while the warmth of the congregation may have much to do with the senior pastor, First Church in Phoenix has many other strengths. One is a staff of well-qualified persons who work well together. They model a relational church lifestyle, which motivates and energizes volunteers. For example, if a job needs to be done, the staff members do not seem to feel that any job is beneath them or that "it's not in my job description."

At a time when many United Methodist congregations are not reaching baby boomers and their children, this church has young families in abundance, which accounts for the average age of the congregation, estimated at 33. This youthful average is especially significant for a city so well known for the number of retirees who move there annually. Two features especially attract these young adults—dynamic preaching and excellent children's programs. For example, the weekday school, established in 1962, is accredited by the National Academy of Early Childhood Programs and has received an Award of Excellence from the city of Phoenix.

Currently, 195 children (ages three through kindergarten) are enrolled in the day school, and there is a waiting list. The curriculum includes music, art, literature, science, creative play, language development, and field trips. Obviously, the school is a great port of entry into the church for many young families.

In addition, a licensed child care program is open five days a week, 7:30 A.M. to 5:30 P.M., throughout the entire year. Children, aged four months to five years, are enrolled. Their flexible schedule allows children to come daily, once or twice weekly, or even on a 24-hour notice for church members, if space is available.

The Sunday school for children is filled to overflowing. An effort is currently being made by the work area on education to encourage more parents to bring their children to the 11:00 A.M. rather than the 9:30 A.M. Sunday school. As in most churches, the youth program has experienced some ups and downs, but the current group seems solidly based and enthusiastic.

Another obvious strength of the church is the music program. Though much more traditional than in many growing churches, its strength is in excellence and the number and variety of the choirs. There are two adult choirs, one madrigal group, two adult handbell choirs, a men's quartet, a senior adult choir, a youth choir, and two children's choirs. Special musical events occur during Advent and Lent. In addition, there is usually a spring concert, a youth choir trip and musical, and organ concerts.

A growing number of persons within First Church have experienced spiritual renewal through annual renewal retreats led by the senior pastor. These experiences make for vitality and authenticity, which is evident in talking with members. Renewal also accounts for the acceptance that visitors feel as they participate in the life of the church. As individuals experience this church's freedom, they find it easier to extend God's love and acceptance to others.

A less tangible strength is the history of this fine church, which extends back to 1881, when Phoenix was incorporated as a town. In actuality, the Methodist Episcopal Church had been loosely organized seven years earlier by a small, bold group of pioneers. These people had braved the heat and drought of the desert, believing that under the guidance of God they could tame the desert and enable it to bloom for those who would come after them.

Indeed, this seed of faith and determined effort seems to have been passed from generation to generation in this church, allowing the congregation to remain stable in the midst of economic depression, war, and social upheavals. This spirit motivated the congregation in 1950 to move from its location in downtown Phoenix as the population center of the city moved northward.

Their present Asbury Hall and educational building were constructed in 1952, and the beautiful contemporary sanctuary was erected in 1957. These buildings are highly visible on a heavily traveled thoroughfare of uptown Phoenix.

If the congregation's expressed needs for more parking, expanded facilities, and increased ministries are met with the same spirit of faith, determination, and creativity that characterized their predecessors, they can believe with Browning that "the best is yet to be."

CENTRAL UNITED PROTESTANT CHURCH

RICHLAND, WASHINGTON

Norman Lawson, Senior Pastor

Perhaps there is no such thing as an average United Methodist church, but Central United Protestant Church in Richland, Washington, is even less average than others. For example, at a time when many people were losing their jobs and moving away from Richland, the church continued to grow. Much of this unusual growth came under the innovative and popular 17½-year ministry of Joe Harding. Fortunately for the church, Harding was followed by Norman Lawson. Though different in administrative style, the philosophy of ministry and their love of people is quite similar. Also it is fortunate for the church that from the beginning the caliber of lay leadership has been superior.

In addition, Central Church is different from most other United Methodist churches in that its first building was provided by the United States government as a Protestant chapel in 1943 for the scientists, engineers, and others who came to participate in the Manhattan Project on the Hanford Reservation. In fact, the entire town of Richland was government built. At the end of World War II, the Roman Catholic chapel was deeded to the Catholic Church and the Protestant chapel to the Methodist Church because the majority of its participants were Methodists.

Even to this day, there is a strong interdenominational climate in the church. "We don't talk much about denomination," said one layman whose early background was American Baptist. "We're Christians first and Methodist second." They are, however, important to and supportive of the United Methodist connectional system. The three ordained clergy of the 23-member staff are United Methodist and are appointed by the bishop and cabinet. A fourth ordained pastor, who is Baptist, heads the Christian Counseling Service.

Perhaps the wide diversity of religious background, the cosmopolitan nature of members (they are well educated, widely traveled, and come from different sections of the country), and the strength and popularity of current and past senior pastors account for the openness of the congregation. A marvelous acceptance of new people and an amazing willingness to try new ideas result in myriad ministries.

An excellent example of their openness is the number of weekend worship services—five. The first is held on Saturday evening at 6:00. Members wear what they like, and much singing takes place at this informal service. Though the sermon is the same for each of the services, there is no choir for the Saturday night service, but always special music. A core group of 70 people is usually in attendance. Others come from time to time, especially when they need to be out of town on Sunday.

The first worship service on Sunday is a rise and shine service, which is attended mainly by young families. At this service a children's message is given, and children act as acolytes. This service is 45 minutes because most of these people will be in Sunday school at 9:00.

The largest attendance, about 600, is for the rejoice service, which is held in the fellowship hall at 9:15. The pastor does not wear a robe; there is a choir of young adults; and the music is contemporary with guitar, piano, and drum accompaniment. A sense of celebration, excitement, and freedom is experienced in this service, which appeals to persons in varying age groups.

About 400 persons, again of varying ages, attend the 11:00 festival service, which is more traditional than the others. The pastor is robed; the music is majestic; and more liturgy is included. Even so, there is an ambience of warmth, and visitors are recognized and welcomed. Applause is open and spontaneous.

The Sunday evening praise and Bible teaching service is held at 6:30 and is charismatic in nature. It includes forty-five minutes of singing, Bible teaching, and emphasis on prayers for healing. An average of 40 attends. In all of these services, a great emphasis is placed upon music. Good music is possible because of the superior music staff, headed by Steve Harter who is Texas-born, Scarritt-trained, and has been at Central Church for nine years. According to laity, Harter connects with people, especially with members of the 13 choirs, orchestra, and brass ensemble.

In addition to music for regular church services, Harter and his staff direct a major work with a 150-voice oratorio choir at Christmas and Easter. Different choirs are used in the four Christmas Eve Candlelight Carol Services, at 5:00, 7:00, 9:00, and 11:00 P.M. Attendance at the four services exceeds 2,400 each year. The choir for older adults (persons 65 and older) presents musicals, such as "Saints Alive" and "Never Too Old for Christmas." Another unusual feature of the church's musical program is a week's music camp for children.

Ministries for children and youth are strong, and are given a special summertime boost from nine interns (carefully screened college and seminary students) who are organized and directed by a coordinator. During an eight-week program, the coordinator and the interns, many of whom are considering full-time service in the church, live in the homes of the members. Members also provide housing for a group of Japanese students who come to the church each summer for a cultural exchange. Lynne Metcalf, program director at the church, works closely with other program staff to coordinate weekly activities and even more closely with Central's large and outstanding singles' ministry. With a constituency of more than 600, the singles' ministry majors in helping singles socialize in a Christian setting. Multiple small groups address specific group needs such as SOS (starting-over singles) and Blended Families (stepfamilies stepping out).

Laity are involved in local missions as well as with a Masai tribe in Kenya. Many members of the church have been to Kenya to help construct church buildings, to teach, and to serve. Central Church's "Kenya Connection" is an innovative way for laity to be directly involved in missions.

There is nothing haphazard about this church. Its long-range planning committee began a "Dream and Possibilities

Workshop" under Harding's leadership and has had the expert guidance of such consultants as Lyle Schaller and Ken Callahan. The committee's goals are threefold: to keep members' minds focused on and to expand their ministries in worship, evangelism, and mission.

Central Protestant United Church in Richland, Washington, is a glorious example of the Body of Christ at work in today's world. The church takes seriously the great commission of Christ and seeks to live it out in loving ways. Watching the church at work calls forth the tribute—"To God be the glory."

GLIDE MEMORIAL UNITED METHODIST CHURCH

SAN FRANCISCO, CALIFORNIA

Cecil Williams, Senior Pastor

In the movie *The Sound of Music*, sisters at the Austrian abbey ask themselves the following questions about the free-spirited nun named Maria: "How do you solve a problem like Maria? How do you catch a rainbow in your hand?"

After visiting Glide Memorial United Methodist Church in San Francisco, one of the fastest growing churches of the Western Jurisdiction, a visitor is likely to ask: "How can you possibly describe the ministry of a church like Glide? How can you catch in words its spirit of celebration and of outreach, and its bedrock commitment to Jesus' reminder 'inasmuch as you do it unto one of the least of these, you do it unto me'?" The answer, of course, is that one can't describe the church adequately; it must be experienced.

From the moment a person walks into the facility, one can recognize that the church is fulfilling the dream of Elizabeth (Lizzie) Glide, who established the church in 1930 in memory of her husband. Her dream was that the church would be a "house of prayer for all people." Today, people of all races, religious affiliations, and socioeconomic backgrounds participate in ministries at Glide. Though her dream may have been envisioned somewhat differently, her words have become a reality.

Fortunately, the trust funds left by Mrs. Glide have been wisely invested. These funds provide for the operation and maintenance of the building, and salaries for both program and administrative staff. Actually, all the ministries at Glide—from feeding 2,000 hungry and homeless people a day, to counseling, to support groups, to day care, to creative arts—are run by a staff of 40 persons and a significant corps of 100 to 150 volunteers per day.

The Evelyn and Walter Haas, Jr. Fund awarded a grant

to Glide for a volunteer coordinator. Since Kristie Jacobs took that position in 1985, volunteerism has increased by 95 percent. She reports: "Volunteers come from all over the Bay area. Individuals and campus, civic, and church groups want to make a difference in the lives of the poor. Also volunteers come from the ranks of the homeless, those whom Glide feeds, because they want to give something back. Without the volunteer force, Glide would be unable to serve the more than one million people who come through our doors with a variety of needs."

In 1988, Jan Mirikitani, Glide's program director since 1969, was named "Woman of the Year" by the California State Assembly. She was honored for having created an arts program that integrates dance, theater, creative writing, and music into the 22 other programs that serve the poor and homeless of San Francisco. Also, on April 7, 1988, Mirikitani and Cecil Williams, senior pastor and catalyst for the growth and vitality of the church, were awarded the University of California's highest honor, given in recognition for their outstanding contribution to health, education, and public service. They were awarded this honor for their leadership in meeting the needs of the disadvantaged, particularly in the Tenderloin area of the city.

Indeed, though Glide's staff includes people of unusual competence, it is Williams whose leadership has enabled the church to grow from a membership of 332 in 1966 to become one of the largest United Methodist congregations in northern California with more than 1,850 members. Williams preaches at the now world-famous Glide Celebration each Sunday morning at 9:00 and 11:00. The events are a unique multimedia mixture of music, singing, and speaking. They feature the Glide Ensemble, the Change Band, and an exciting light show. Hundreds of people from around the world attend the Glide Celebration.

A minister of liberation, Williams teaches and preaches the importance of learning to "break free." Many of the church's programs are designed to help people break free from alcohol, drugs, and abusive and oppressive situations. The newest ministry is called "Hope Without Dope," which is a street-focused education and information program designed to arm potential victims against crack abuse, as well as to help those already addicted to overcome it. The program includes educational meetings, support groups, medical help (through the Haight-Ashbury Free Clinic), and a "Facts on Crack" brochure, which catalogues in graphic form the physical and emotional devastation caused by the drug.

Mo's Kitchen is well known throughout the San Francisco community. Mo Bernstein, a prominent businessman, is one of the most respected leaders in the city and is the chief benefactor of Mo's Kitchen. The kitchen is located in the basement of the church, and three meals are served daily to over 2,000 destitute persons. Special meals are prepared to celebrate holidays throughout the year. Over 6,000 persons are served on Thanksgiving, Christmas, and Easter. Insisting on high quality in everything he does, Bernstein says, "We serve only fresh food." He is grateful for the large participation of the members of the Bay community. For example, Safeway and Lucky grocery chains donate food; Lou Giraudo gives French bread; and Transamerica Insurance Company has turned off its Christmas lights and given the saved money to Glide instead. In a copy of "Mo's Newsletter," Bernstein is quoted as saying, "We are seeing in this giving the only thing that will alleviate hunger: a spirit of sharing and thinking of the needs of others."

The University of the Street has been created at Glide where people from the street and academia develop and offer programs for learning, liberation, and empowerment. One of the University's programs, "Taking the Church to the Street," is an annual summer institute in which clergy and laity come together to learn to meet the needs of the poor. The Crisis Center offers emergency counseling, information, and referral assistance from 9:00 A.M. to 5:00 P.M. each weekday, and provides telephone numbers for weekend referrals.

The children's program will undoubtedly have long-lasting results. It includes early childhood education, a tutorial program for children of all ages, and a parent's support group. The children participate in field trips, creative writing, drama, cooking, arts and crafts, as well as Christian education.

On visiting this unique church in the heart of one of

America's great cities, it is easy to hear the words of Christ echo through the halls: "I was hungry and you gave me food, naked and you clothed me, sick and in prison and you came unto me. . . . Enter thou into the joy of thy Lord."